PREVIOUS BOOK BY CHRISTOPHER COLWELL

*Impact: How Assistant Principals
Can Be High Performing Leaders*
(Rowman & Littlefield, March 2015)

Mission-Driven Leadership

Understanding the Challenges Facing Schools Today

Christopher Colwell

ROWMAN & LITTLEFIELD
Lanham • Boulder • New York • London

Published by Rowman & Littlefield
A wholly owned subsidiary of
The Rowman & Littlefield Publishing Group, Inc.
4501 Forbes Boulevard, Suite 200, Lanham, Maryland 20706
https://rowman.com

Unit A, Whitacre Mews, 26-34 Stannary Street, London SE11 4AB, United Kingdom

Copyright © 2018 by Christopher Colwell

All rights reserved. No part of this book may be reproduced in any form or by any electronic or mechanical means, including information storage and retrieval systems, without written permission from the publisher, except by a reviewer who may quote passages in a review.

British Library Cataloguing in Publication Information Available

Library of Congress Cataloging-in-Publication Data

Names: Colwell, Christopher, author.
Title: Mission-driven leadership : understanding the challenges facing schools today / Christopher Colwell.
Description: Lanham, Maryland : Rowman & Littlefield, [2018] | Includes bibliographical references.
Identifiers: LCCN 2017053648 (print) | LCCN 2018002360 (ebook) | ISBN 9781475836240 (Electronic) | ISBN 9781475836226 (cloth : alk. paper) | ISBN 9781475836233 (pbk. : alk. paper)
Subjects: LCSH: Educational leadership--United States. | School management and organization--United States.
Classification: LCC LB2805 (ebook) | LCC LB2805 .C614 2018 (print) | DDC 371.2--dc23
LC record available at https://lccn.loc.gov/2017053648

∞ ™ The paper used in this publication meets the minimum requirements of American National Standard for Information Sciences Permanence of Paper for Printed Library Materials, ANSI/NISO Z39.48-1992.

Printed in the United States of America

To Rylee and Amelia

Contents

Foreword		ix
Preface		xi
Acknowledgments		xiii
Introduction		xv
1	Getting to Tier 3: A Journey Worth Taking	1
2	The Leader as Manager (Tier 1)	7
3	The Leader as Instructional Expert (Tier 2)	15
4	The Leader as Interpersonal Expert (Tier 3)	23
5	Get to 50 Percent Tier 2 and Tier 3 Behavior	31
6	Brush Off the Chips	45
7	Reduce Position Power Behavior	55
8	Find and Use a Mission Voice	67
9	Trust Down the Organization	81
10	Lead Up the Organization	93
11	Focus on Process	105
12	Dance with the Dancers	115
13	Dance with the Silent	123
14	Avoid Isolation and Embrace Inquiry	135
15	Sustaining Tier 3 Leadership	143
Bibliography		151

About the Author 157

Foreword

Why is it that those dedicated to the art of leadership are naturally drawn to leadership blogs, articles, and books? It is as though we are forever on a quest for the holy grail of leadership. The repetition of reading about leadership styles and practices is a testament that the reader seeks to improve his or her craft.

A few years ago, Chris Colwell mentioned to me his research on the effective behaviors of school leaders, which ultimately resulted in a book destined to be referenced often by school leaders. Just the title of the book itself is intriguing, because it promises practical insights for successful leadership. *Mission-Driven Leadership: Understanding the Challenges Facing Schools Today* is a powerful guide to building and leading high-performing teams in schools and districts as the twenty-first century moves forward.

Chris Colwell has always been held in high regard in Volusia County, Florida. Throughout his career, words such as *brilliant*, *innovative*, and *forward thinking* were commonly used when his name was mentioned. To rising administrators, he had this aura of…the man, the myth, the legend. The air was almost let out of that tire for me when at a holiday luncheon I saw Chris donning a sombrero and shaking maracas while leading the crowd in Christmas carols, and it did not get any better when he led sixty-five principals in a winding conga line.

I came to realize that his jocularity was an extension of his personality, and this event taught me a lot about Chris as a leader. He had reverent power among principals because he understood the challenges of our work and nudged us forward in an age of increasing accountability, but he also would never miss an opportunity to make us laugh when making a point. In *Mission-Driven Leadership*, Chris is nudging education leaders forward once again.

American education still holds on to many of the trappings of its past, yet it has changed over the last century and the demand for change continues to accelerate. In the first chapter of *Mission-Driven Leadership,* Chris explains the evolution of school systems over the last century and what has been required from leadership. Schools in the early to mid-twentieth century were reminiscent of the era of industry and manufacturing.

Administrators were expected to manage schools with efficiency and produce workers for the local industries. During the age of *Sputnik* and throughout the second half of the twentieth century, curriculum and teaching methodologies were called into question; therefore, school administrators were expected to have expert power as *instructional leaders,* as well as the ability to manage a school site with efficiency. As the twenty-first century progresses, Chris makes the case that school administrators need just as much now to be experts in interpersonal skills in order to propel the mission of the school forward through the work of powerful teams.

Because I am the superintendent of a school district with hundreds of school and district administrators, *Mission-Driven Leadership: Understanding the Challenges Facing Schools Today* resonates with me, because the book is both balanced and practical. Each chapter identifies the barriers that must be overcome and behavioral insights that lead to high-impact leadership. One chapter is dedicated to each of the ten behaviors and is set in a context familiar to educators. Chris proves once again that he is a teacher first, by including an interesting conclusion to each chapter with the statement *Today Is a Good Day to...,* followed by concrete suggestions to implement into the school leader's daily practice. Chris Colwell has written a guidebook that will be used and treasured by practitioners.

By nature, educators believe they can change the future every day, because they are change agents in students' lives. It is the responsibility of the teams at each school site and throughout the district to create an environment in which that can happen. Education leaders and those pursuing such leadership will gravitate to and find great value in *Mission-Driven Leadership: Understanding the Challenges Facing Schools Today* because of the commonsense and pragmatic strategies within its pages. After reading this gift, you will discover that you have found the holy grail of leadership.

Tom Russell
   Superintendent of Schools
   Volusia County Public Schools
   DeLand, Florida

Preface

Education leaders, whether school-based or district-based, face ever-increasing challenges and responsibilities. The need for school leaders in the twenty-first century to possess a wide array of leadership skills, talents, and dispositions is without debate. Over the last one hundred years, there have been several evolving schools of thought regarding what skills are needed by the school leader.

Over time, the knowledge, skills, and dispositions expected from leaders in the education sector have only grown in scope and complexity. Leadership development during the early twentieth century consisted primarily of training school leaders as efficiency experts who could manage the operation of the school "assembly line" to meet the growing demand for a literate and trainable labor force for the developing Industrial Age.

In the later decades of the century, the expanding complexity of school curriculum, along with a deeper understanding of the skills needed for teachers to teach effectively, resulted in a focus on school leaders needing to possess expert power as "instructional leaders." Today there is a growing consensus that high-performing school leaders must be also be experts in a third tier of leadership, interpersonal skills.

The competencies that are considered essential to high performance for leaders of educational institutions continue to expand in both number and complexity. Each of these skill sets and dispositions are necessary for the modern school leader, but none of these abilities (management skills, instructional skills, or interpersonal skills) are sufficient, in and of themselves, for as an educational leader's high performance in facing today's school challenges.

Mission is designed for the practicing educational leader who seeks new strategies to build trust, commitment, and a common mission for all members of the organization as a primary leadership goal. The leadership strategies and mind-sets outlined in this book can be used successfully by educators serving at any level within the organization, regardless of title or job scope. *Mission* is also designed for the educator who is pursuing new leadership opportunities or who wishes to expand their influence on the organization and its stakeholders.

Thomas Jefferson said, "Show me a nation that is both ignorant and free, and I will show you a nation that never has been and never will be." What happens in our nation's schools matters, not only to our children, but also to our country.

The quality of our educational system, and the ability of our educational leaders to understand and solve the challenges facing schools today, requires leaders who can build and sustain team-oriented, mission-driven school cultures. The ability of our twenty-first-century school leaders will determine, to a great extent, the overall quality of our society and our capacity to solve the complex challenges of the twenty-first century. *Mission-Driven Leadership: Understanding the Challenges Facing Schools Today* is written to provide education leaders everywhere with straightforward strategies that make a difference in the ability of the leader to have an impact: to matter.

Acknowledgments

I have been blessed to work with many mission-driven leaders during my more than forty years working in the education field. To all the leaders, at the university and at the P–12 level, who have mentored and inspired me, a special thank-you. Thank you for making a difference in my life and in the lives of children.

To the teachers and colleagues who have informed my thinking on the nature of leadership as a team-oriented, mission-driven enterprise, thank you for your expertise and feedback on this book. To Joyce Mundy, Lou Sabina, Patrick Coggins, Glen Epley, Rajni Shankar-Brown, and Deb Touchton, thank you for your work in teaching the next generation of school leaders. To all of my colleagues at Stetson University who have supported my scholarly activities and have provided me with assistance on this project whenever needed, a special thank-you. Thanks to Superintendents Jim Surratt, Joan Kowal, Bill Hall, Margaret Smith, Walt Griffin, Tom Russell, and Jim Tager, for your support and inspiration over the years.

Lastly, a very special thank-you to my wife and inspiration, Monique Colwell, and my mother, Ann Colwell, for all of the encouragement, love, and support.

Introduction

Mission-Driven Leadership: Understanding the Challenges Facing Schools Today examines the skills and behaviors that high-impact school leaders need to cultivate in order to achieve their organizational mission and make a profound difference in the lives of the students they serve. In an age of ever-increasing complexity and demand on educational leaders, *Mission* examines a specific set of leadership behaviors that, when implemented with fidelity on a daily basis, will result in high performance for all P–12 leaders, regardless of rank or position in the organization.

Part 1 ("Moving to Tier 3 Leadership") examines the three (3) common tiers, or job descriptions/expectations, that educational leaders are either trapped into by their own behaviors or by the duties and responsibilities assigned to them by supervisors and stakeholders throughout the organization. These lower-tier leadership functions can consume the leader's time and energy and are often viewed as the skills upon which the leader will be evaluated by supervisors, making it even more difficult to break out of Tier 1 management leadership. The limitations to serving exclusively as a manager are not obvious. After all, if an organization is not well run, well managed, how can success occur?

Mission-Driven Leadership goes on to examine how leaders can impact the organization in more profound and sustainable ways. Rather than just ensuring a well-run, well-managed, efficient school or school district, specific leadership strategies are explored to help the organization move toward its core mission: making a profound difference in the lives of the students being served.

Part 2 ("The Daily Top 10") examines ten (10) specific leadership behaviors that can be implemented on a daily basis regardless of the leader's assignment within the organization or the level of education the leader is serving. Whether the leader is a first-year assistant principal or the superintendent of a large school district, whether the leader is working with elementary, middle, or high school teachers and students, the leadership behaviors examined in this section ground the school leader in simple behaviors and protocols that can be replicated over time and will have a profound impact on the leader's ability to build a team-oriented, mission-driven organization.

Each chapter in part 2 examines a specific leadership behavior that can be implemented without additional training or the need to secure the commitment of others. The strategies examined in this section are grounded in research and designed to prioritize Tier 2 and Tier 3 leadership behaviors as described in Part 1 of the text. Specific examples of the behaviors in action are described, along with a review of the challenges that the high-impact leader must overcome in order to implement these behaviors consistently and with fidelity.

Specific behavior traps and solutions to those traps are also described for each of the ten (10) leadership behaviors discussed. Each chapter concludes with a section entitled "Today Is a Good Day To . . ." with a list, followed by a brief description of daily behaviors that will support each of the ten strategies described in part 2 of the book.

Mission concludes with a discussion regarding leadership sustainability. How do leaders, working at the highest levels, maintain excellence in the work and an ongoing commitment to the value of the work over sustained periods of time? Specific strategies for sustaining excellence as a leader who can perform at the highest levels of all tiers of leadership are discussed in this final chapter.

Chapter One

Getting to Tier 3

A Journey Worth Taking

Leaders matter. Any complex organization requires effective leadership in order to succeed. Schools and school districts are certainly no exception. Next to the impact of the classroom teacher, perhaps no position has more capacity to influence and improve the performance of our nations' schools than school leaders. From the first-year assistant principal to the veteran district superintendent of schools, leaders matter.

Perhaps the quickest way to change the direction of a school in terms of performance or culture is to change the leadership in the school. Great teachers cannot function to their full ability in school or district environments that are led by leaders who do not have the skill and will to be high-impact leaders of teams on a common and important mission. Conversely, when a school or school district is led by a leader who is a skilled manager, a skilled instructional leader, and a skilled interpersonal leader, the capacity for positive outcomes and an organizational culture focused on making a difference in the lives of students is greatly enhanced.

Any examination of a school or school district that is going through a leadership change due to retirement or reorganization will show stakeholders throughout the organization who are anxious or nervous about the next occupant of any leadership position. Why do so many stakeholders share this level of anxiety and uncertainty? Stakeholders both within and without the organization recognize instinctively that the leader's behaviors, attitudes, skill sets, and mission goals will have a significant impact, for better or for worse, on the organization as a whole.

Chapter 1

HIGH-IMPACT LEADERS MATTER

So, what does it mean to be an impactful school leader in the twenty-first century? The complexity of the roles and responsibilities of the school principal in the twenty-first century has grown exponentially over the last few decades (Rousmaniere, 2013). The list of responsibilities, tasks, and demands that school leaders face on a daily basis can be daunting. The wide scope of responsibilities, the hundreds of daily decisions, big and small, the demands on the leader's time that school leaders face each day are only growing with each passing year.

With the transition in American education from a focus on equal access to education, which dominated the education narrative for much of the twentieth century (Herrera, 2004; Kluger, 2011), to the more recent focus on the quality of the education that students are actually receiving, the focus on the quality of teachers and leaders in K–12 settings has come under extreme scrutiny, not only in America but around the world (Dinham, 2013; Peng et.al., 2014). Today it is no longer enough to have a school in which every student has the opportunity to attend and learn. Today's schools are also being held accountable for ensuring that all students have, in fact, actually learned.

As the responsibilities and expectations for school leaders has grown, there is a growing need for both school districts and universities to reexamine the skills and attributes that high-performing school and district leaders must have in order to be successful in the twenty-first century. Perhaps the question every leader must be able to answer deals more with the attributes the leader possesses than the training, or experience, the leader has.

Universities training school leaders, and districts that continue that training and ongoing professional development, spend a great deal of time, and correctly so, building the capacity of the leader to have the skill sets and expertise necessary to be both an efficient manager and an instructional leader. What is often given short shrift or ignored altogether is a very fundamental question, a question every leader must be able to answer with clarity: "Why should anyone be led by me?"

Leaders who answer this question with examples of how position power is used effectively, how well managed the school or organization is, or even how much expert power the leader is bringing to the organization are not providing answers or examples that, in and of themselves, lead to mission-oriented, high-functioning teams. Leaders who cannot demonstrate, in word and deed, why followers can believe in and trust the leader's capacity to build teams that are committed to a common and meaningful mission will not succeed in the increasingly complex environment that is twenty-first-century education. It is the mission that matters. It is the mission that motivates.

While our education calendar may continue to operate on an agrarian calendar, our economy and the skills and dispositions high school graduates need to succeed are no longer connected to an agrarian economy. While our school day and organizational structure may continue to operate on an assembly-line, mass-production model, our graduates must have the skills necessary for the new Digital and Information Age.

Our modern school systems now operate in what the United States military has described as a VUCA environment: that is, an environment that is volatile, uncertain, complex, and ambiguous (Bennet & Lemoine, 2014). Any leader or observer of the modern school system would agree that volatility, uncertainty, complexity, and ambiguity are accurate descriptions of both the daily life of school educators and leaders, as well as good descriptions of how our society's ever-changing policies and goals feel to those in the field.

Twenty-first-century schools are volatile. That is to say, in many ways our modern school systems function on the edge of sustainability and certainty. Chronic underfunding; massive amounts of local, state, and federal regulation and oversight; shifting societal demands and expectations; and ever-increasing demands for higher student achievement and accountability represent just a few of the many significant factors that make daily life in the school, for both students and teachers alike, a volatile environment.

In addition to being volatile environments, twenty-first-century schools are also filled with uncertainty. Educators at all levels of the organization are uncertain about job security, about financial stability, about consistency in regulations, and about expected outcomes and organizational goals, just to name a few significant stressors on stakeholders. For the same reasons just listed, it is increasingly difficult for school leaders to plan strategically over a period of years. How can long-term strategic planning occur when there is so much uncertainty about long-term organizational structures, goals, and activities to meet those goals?

In an era of increasing uncertainty, teachers and leaders, students and parents, feel buffeted from one reform movement to the next, from one change in administration with different priorities to the next. One would be hard-pressed to find a group of educators at any level who would agree that they could count on, with certainty, any aspect of how their work will look or how their work will be measured even two to three years into the future.

In addition to being volatile and uncertain, twenty-first-century schools are increasingly complex. One would be hard pressed to find any other sector in our society that has so many different stakeholders who are both actively involved in the organization and hold strong opinions regarding how the organization should function. Almost every American has been through school and thus feels a certain sense of expertise regarding how schools should operate and what is working or not working within the school systems in which they live and in the nation as a whole.

What other sectors of our society operate under so many jurisdictions with so many regulations and with so much at stake? Modern schools operate under the direction of local school boards, state boards of education, as well as a multitude of federal regulatory bodies. Politicians at every level are actively engaged in oversight and regulatory reform. Whether it is how to evaluate teacher performance, what to teach, how to evaluate student performance, or any other number of high-stakes components of the school system, the complexity of the modern American school is unparalleled in our history.

Finally, twenty-first-century schools operate in environments that are ambiguous. That is, it is hard for stakeholders and educators to see and understand what a successful education looks like. In the manufacturing sector, success can be measured in units delivered and profit margins attained. The agriculture sector can measure crop yield. In education, however, success is harder to quantify and can come in many guises. Success may be a high test score, but that is far from a certainty. Success may be graduating with a degree. Success may be helping a student cope with bullying, social isolation, or issues at home. Success may be helping a student discover their inherent self-worth or a passion for a particular vocation or avocation. In reality, all of these outcomes matter.

In a society that cannot come to consensus regarding what it even means to be "educated," it is hard to assess, without a great deal of ambiguity and uncertainty, whether "successful" education is occurring.

In these complex and dynamic education settings, the skills and attributes that school leaders possess must be able not only to handle the VUCA environment in which they work, but also be able to thrive and build certainty and stability into the system despite the environment. This type of leadership requires more than managerial skill or pedagogical expertise. This type of leadership requires interpersonal skills built on the foundation of a meaningful mission that influences stakeholders, and builds high-functioning teams throughout the organization (Bligh, Pearce, & Kohles, 2006).

For much of the latter part of the twentieth century and the early part of the twenty-first century, the demands on school leaders transitioned from a focus on the leader as an effective manager using the power of the position to run the school as a smooth and efficient system, to a focus on the leader as an instructional expert who understands teaching and learning and the instructional frameworks widely accepted as modern pedagogical best practice (Danielson, 2011; Marzano, 2005).

While position power, granted by the title of leader, may have been all that was needed for yesterday's school leader, the use of position power to manage the organization, and even a reliance on expert power to lead the organization in ways that reflect the best practices and the best thinking in the field, seems wholly inadequate to the modern demands of leadership development (Zenger & Folkman, 2002).

INFLUENCE MATTERS

An emerging area of focus in understanding what makes a leader truly impactful deals with a third level of leadership behaviors that do not replace position power (level one) or expert power (level two), but are seen as a new prerequisite set of skills that high-performing leaders must also have. This third level of leadership skills is the ability to influence others (Pink, 2014). This level of leadership skill deals with interpersonal skill development (Zenger & Folkman, 2002). It is the ability of the leader to develop teams around a meaningful mission and build positive school cultures and climates that support that mission.

In this Level Three environment, it is the development of the school leaders' ability to use interpersonal skills in ways that are viewed by stakeholders as charismatic or mission driven that must be in place for impactful school leadership to occur. This mission-driven leadership centers around the ability of the leader to influence others and empower others also to be leaders. In this context, the Tier 3 leader is a leader of teams of leaders.

Tier 3 leaders recognize that it is the development of high-performing teams of leaders that enhances the capacity for meaningful change. It is the leader's ability to communicate, to motivate, to influence, and to inspire large teams of stakeholders that characterizes the Tier 3 leader. These behaviors are often described as "charismatic behaviors." The charisma of the high-performing Tier 3 leader, however, is not rooted in the extroversion of the leader, in the ability of the leader to be a great public speaker, but in the ability of the leader to be mission driven and influence others to believe, not in the leader, but in the mission the leader espouses.

This ability of the leader to infuse meaning into the organization characterizes the Tier 3 leader. This ability to harness interpersonal skills to develop others and build coalitions around important missions can be developed. There is a set of behaviors that, when implemented with fidelity on a daily basis, can result in Tier 3 leadership behavior and the increased likelihood that meaningful and significant impact on the primary mission of the school will occur. These behaviors can be learned and reasonably implemented despite the tremendous demands and strain on the school leader's time.

While no article, book, or seminar series can cover the large and complex set of behaviors that define excellent leadership, there are several fundamental behaviors and skill sets that, when implemented with fidelity and strived for on a daily basis, increase the likelihood for leaders to succeed.

These behaviors impact how the leader spends the day, uses power, and communicates with colleagues and stakeholders at all levels of the organization. These behaviors inform how the leader prioritizes time, delegates authority and responsibility, and responds to adversity. These behaviors can be successful immediately if the leader has the will and the discipline to both self-check their current standing against the behaviors suggested, and make the commitment to implement the behaviors on a daily basis.

It is not enough for leaders to recognize the attributes necessary for these behaviors, they must also be acted on each day. These high-impact leadership behaviors are not, however, behaviors associated with the leader as a manager or with the leader as an instructional leader. Instead these behaviors require the leader to function on a daily basis as an interpersonal expert.

So, what does it mean to be a Tier 1 Manager Leader, and a Tier 2 Instructional Leader, as well as a Tier 3 Interpersonal Leader? First, it is important to understand that leaders are made, not born. Or perhaps it is more accurate to say that leaders are developed, coached, self-taught, and mentored. In many ways, it is through the determination of the leader's will to consistently improve, and the ability of the leader to live a mission-driven life, focused on lifelong learning not just for others, but for the leader himself, that determines the degree to which leaders are successful.

Second, it is important for the leader to understand and differentiate between management leadership behavior, expert instructional leadership behavior, and interpersonal leadership behavior. Third, the leader must be willing to give Tier 3 interpersonal leadership activity and Tier 2 instructional leadership activity an equal footing with the leader's priorities for management activity and success.

No leader gets to Tier 3 by accident. No leader gets to Tier 3 without having a solid foundation in the skill sets and attributes that make up Tier 1 and Tier 2 leadership. Most importantly, no leader gets to Tier 3 without having a fundamental understanding of, and belief in, the value of the mission itself. Tier 3 leaders are mission-driven leaders. Tier 3 leaders understand the mission, can articulate the mission, and value the mission above all else in the organizations they lead.

For too many leaders, the time needed, and the emphasis placed, on management activity and instructional activity leaves little room or capacity for the leader to function as a builder of teams on a common mission.

Tier 3 leaders do not abandon Tier 1 or Tier 2 behaviors. These leaders continue to prioritize, organize, and lead in ways that ensure that these fundamental prerequisites for organizational success are in place. By building teams of leaders and distributing leadership responsibility and authority to leadership teams, the high-performing leader can dedicate more time to Tier 3 behaviors while still attending to Tier 1 and Tier 2 behaviors.

These Tier 3 leaders still recognize the importance of having a solid foundation in the skills needed to be a leader who can manage the organization effectively (Tier 1) and having the same solid foundation in the skills needed to be a leader who is seen as an expert, in this case an instructional expert (Tier 2). Mission-driven Tier 3 leaders understand and are able to function at high levels in all three areas.

Chapter Two

The Leader as Manager (Tier 1)

It is important to recognize that the historical design of our teaching and learning model in the United States is built upon the organizational model of the early Industrial Age with an emphasis on mass production using an assembly line that is efficiently managed.

When the Model T rolled off the line on October 1, 1908, not only had the Industrial Age begun, but the industrialization of schools was born, as well. Educators hoped that the efficiencies of the assembly line and mass production that made the Model T a modern marvel could be transferred to the education sector, where the demand for a large educated workforce was sure to increase in the new Industrial Age. As a result, the standardization of the Industrial Age was not limited to automotive plants or other sectors of manufacturing, but to our emerging standardized school system, as well.

As early as the late 1800s, the need for some type of standardization for our curricular scope and sequence was under way. The Committee of Ten in 1892, consisting of some of the most preeminent minds in the educational field of the day, was commissioned by the National Education Association and chaired by Charles Eliot, the president of Harvard, to, among other things, determine at what age specific school subjects should be taught and how many years and how many hours a week should any particular subject be taught.

The report, now almost 125 years old, included the recommendation to develop a standardized school system consisting of twelve years of education. The twelve-year sequence would consist of eight years of elementary school and four years of high school.

By expanding the role of secondary education to include a curricula not just for those few college-bound students at the time studying Latin and Greek classic curricula, but also for those students for whom a high school diploma would be a terminal degree designed to prepare them to be successful in the workplace, home, and in society at large, the recommendations of the NEA's Committee of Ten had a profound impact on the purpose and design of the school system that was being built for a new century and a new economy (Meyer, 1968; Ornstein & Levine, 1993).

The Committee of Ten also recommended that every subject taught in high school be offered in the same way so as to provide an equal opportunity for all students to master the subject. Finally, each and every subject taught would be offered five days a week and for the same amount of time each day. If mathematics was offered for sixty minutes each day, then science would be sixty minutes per day, as well as social studies, physical education, and so on. Our education system was thus born out of the Industrial Age of the early twentieth century.

The educators necessary to lead this new education model had to be trained in, and excel at, the same skills that high-performing factory managers had. These leaders needed to understood systems planning and the value of efficiency and organizational management in a well-run bureaucratic system.

Over the last century, our education assembly line has remained remarkably consistent in its design and infrastructure. While almost every other facet of modern life has evolved significantly over the last one hundred years, some to the degree of being almost unrecognizable from the status of even thirty years ago, much less one hundred years ago, the members of the Committee of Ten would clearly recognize the organization and structure of today's twenty-first-century schools. The scope and sequence of our "modern" curriculum, our school calendar, and our daily schedule would all fit comfortably into the recommendations they made back at the turn of the twentieth century.

With the inclusion of kindergarten as a common entry point for today's student, the assembly line has grown from twelve stations to thirteen stations. Our economy and workforce have moved from the Agricultural Age to the Manufacturing Age to the Digital Age; we just forgot to move our schools along with it. The knowledge base we expect all students to master and to which we hold all educators accountable has certainly grown exponentially over the decades.

This trend for student mastery of more content and for mastering that content earlier in the education K–12 cycle has only increased with each passing year. The amount of standardized testing and societal expectations regarding what it means to be a successful high school graduate has also certainly grown over the decades.

WHAT IS MODERN?

Yet in many profound ways, our modern system for educating children is not modern at all (Colwell, 2017). The assembly line model designed for a manufacturing age is not conducive to what we know about how learning occurs or the skill sets and tools students now need for a digital, connected Information Age.

Today's students interact with knowledge and information in very different ways from the children of the 1890s. Human beings develop and learn at different rates of speed, with individuals maturing intellectually at different speeds and with different life experiences. All children do not encounter every skill and subject with the same level of academic readiness (Semrun-Clikeman, 2016). Highly regulated and fixed teaching schedules designed for mass production do not fit well into the individualized needs and readiness levels of many children today.

The amount of content we ask each teacher to teach and each student to learn has certainly grown exponentially over the last one hundred–plus years and the number of standardized assessments in use in our schools has skyrocketed over the last thirty years, but the fundamental design and structure of our school system remains intact as an assembly line designed to mass-produce an educated graduate in a consistent and efficient manner.

As in 1892 and 1908, each station (grade level) in the schools of 2018 are still tasked with delivering specific curriculum built upon the knowledge gained by students at the previous station (grade level). The fact that the amount of knowledge expected to be delivered at each station has increased by leaps and bounds over the decades only exacerbates the disconnect between the modern demands society has placed on the nation's education system and the antiquated system still trying to meet those demands.

TIER 1: THE LEADER AS MANAGER

Still, out of the need to provide an education to all students rather than just the privileged few, a concerted effort to learn from, and use, the efficiencies and management leadership styles needed to run large factories was seen as an appropriate way to expand educational opportunity. In order to run these new factory schools, leaders who had the expertise and skill sets to manage the mass-production of education would be needed. These leaders needed the skills necessary to manage large and complex organizations. As project managers, they needed to be able to ensure efficiency, safety, standardization, and a smooth-running organization.

If the ability for leaders to understand efficiency and consistency within a complex bureaucratic organization was needed for leading factories, the same skills would be valued in leading the new expanding education assembly line.

This need for well-managed schools should not be questioned or taken lightly. Clearly structures are needed in schools in order to manage the distribution of labor, to ensure that management policies are in place and operating smoothly, and to ensure that there is a fundamental level of accountability and responsibility in place throughout the system (Tschannen-Moran, 2009).

The concept of the leader as manager (Tier 1 leadership) is deeply engrained in our traditions and expectations for educational leaders. It is important to note that all mission-driven leaders who have the skill sets and the desire to be Tier 2 expert leaders and Tier 3 mission-driven leaders still need management expertise. The ability to manage the organization well, to lead in ways that ensure organizational safety, efficiency, and goal attainment, are prerequisite skills for leaders whose mission is to truly make a difference in the lives of students (Bush, 2007).

The ability of the school leader to ensure a safe school, the ability to ensure the efficient operation of the school, and the ability to prioritize and delegate duties effectively are all necessary and fundamental to the overall health and success of the organization. Teachers cannot teach and students cannot learn in environments that are not safe and orderly. It is reasonable to argue that student safety is not only a key responsibility of any school leader, but the number-one priority for today's school leader. Teachers cannot teach, students cannot learn, and complex team-oriented activity cannot occur in schools or school systems that are not operating safely and efficiently.

In environments in which financial support and human resource support is scarce, how time is used becomes a critical factor in the overall success of the organization. Schools and districts that are not well managed, that are not running smoothly and efficiently—in short, that are wasting time through needless duplication of efforts in the organization, or in repeating the same mistakes over and over—are systems that never get to the big missions of the organization because they can't manage the small missions of the organization.

The fundamental challenge of Tier 1 leadership is not to minimize the importance of the leader as a skilled manager of complex systems, but not to become consumed by the management of these systems and only be a leader who just manages the organization. The challenge for all education leaders is to be great Tier 1 leaders and be able to serve as high-performing instructional and interpersonal leaders.

Because of the danger of being consumed by the daily operations of a building or a district, perhaps the most important Tier 1 leadership skill is the ability to effectively delegate and prioritize organizational tasks. High-performing managers understand how to delegate not only tasks and activities, but also the authority and responsibility to carry out those tasks and activities.

High-performing managers do not micromanage. They understand that micromanaging too many activities is a waste of leadership time that could be spent leading Tier 2 and Tier 3 activities, and it also has the side effect of reducing the trust of subordinates or a belief by subordinates that their expertise and capacity for excellence are truly valued. If the leader really trusts them, then why is the leader micromanaging and constantly double-checking what is being delegated?

In addition to leaders who don't know how to delegate effectively, leaders who are not skilled at prioritizing are likely to find themselves reacting to events, looking like firefighters responding to one blaze after another rather than looking like proactive leaders who have control of their calendar and how best to use the leaders' most precious asset, time. There will always be fires that need to be extinguished. There will always be real emergencies that disrupt even the most organized and committed leader's calendar.

For too many leaders, however, every unscheduled event or encounter feels like a fire, or an emergency that must be responded to, resulting in a kind of "restricted vision" by the leader (Everard, Morris, & Wilson, 2004). Understanding what truly is an emergency and recognizing tasks that need to be accomplished but are not really emergencies, not really must-act-on-now tasks, are not specifically time-sensitive, or could easily be accomplished by other members of the team, is a necessary skill for any leader wishing to move beyond managing activity only.

For all of the reasons discussed above, Tier 1 leadership, highly effective managing of the school or district, is a necessary prerequisite for leading as an instructional leader and as a mission-driven developer of teams. If the school leader is an expert in teaching and learning, but cannot ensure the smooth and safe operation of the school—in short, cannot manage the school well—true education for all students is unlikely to occur. The physical and emotional safety of all students, faculty, staff, and stakeholders in the building is indeed a compelling condition that must be met by the leader.

If the school leader is an expert in interpersonal skills and team building, but cannot lead a focused, organized, and safe school environment, then no amount of mission-driven behaviors will result in meeting the organization's goals.

Even in climates that are safe, orderly, and efficient, teachers cannot teach and students cannot learn when communication between and among all stakeholders is missing or inconsistent. Systems for how processes are followed, how records are kept, and how decisions are made must be clearly understood by all stakeholders. The management of information and the establishment of clear and consistent channels of communication are also prerequisites for leaders and effective school management.

The need to focus on process is just as important as the need to focus on results. If the processes and systems to achieve difficult outcomes are not in place and understood by everyone, those difficult and complex goals will not be met. The leadership skill of "focusing on process" will be discussed in depth in chapter 11.

The modern education leader operates in an environment of limited resources combined with ever-expanding societal expectations. Today, school and school district leaders must learn how to operate with limited and unstable financial resources. While the school leader may build a strategic plan based on certain budgetary assumptions, there is a high degree of likelihood that those assumptions, unless based on very conservative budget projections, will prove to be unreliable. In what appears to be a never-ending era of financial constraint, the ability of the leader and the leadership team to manage limited resources is critical.

Financial constraints are not the only management issues faced by twenty-first-century education leaders. The number of administrative and support personnel available to the school system is also limited, and in many cases decreasing over time. Today's leader is literally expected to do more with less—less financial support and less human resource support. In these types of environments, the leader who is highly skilled as an effective and high-performing manager is critical.

The ability to lead in ways that maximize efficiency and prioritize what is important, to understand and successfully use Tier 1 skills and ensure the successful management of the operation as a whole, will always be a leadership prerequisite.

No one can be an instructional leader in an organization that is not well managed. No leader can build teams of stakeholders, both within and without the organization, who are focused on mission-driven strategic action if the fundamentals of the organization—for example, safety, stability, consistency in processes, efficiency, clarity—are not in place. The opportunity to be a mission-driven, team-oriented leader is built upon the overall stability and infrastructure of the organization that is supported by leaders and leadership teams with strong managerial skills.

Unfortunately, while the leader as an expert manager may have been sufficient for the first half of the last century, management expertise alone is not sufficient for the modern twenty-first-century leader. A leader who is well trained and able to manage the operational functions and systems of the school, but who does not have the ability to serve as an instructional leader (Tier 2) or serve as a leader of people and of teams on a common mission (Tier 3), cannot be successful in the twenty-first century.

While Tier 1 management skills are necessary, Tier 2 teaching and learning expert skill and Tier 3 people skills are also necessary prerequisites for high-impact leadership. As with many aspects of leadership effectiveness, leadership in the twenty-first century is a question of balance: balance between the time a leader spends managing the daily operations of the school and the time the leader spends serving as an instructional and interpersonal leader. The leader who is 100 percent management oriented, at the expense of instructional and interpersonal leadership, cannot succeed. Likewise, the leader who focuses 100 percent of his efforts on providing instructional leadership and interpersonal team-building leadership, at the expense of ensuring a well-run school or district, cannot succeed, either.

The high-performing leader sets, as a daily goal, to limit management activity to no more than 50 percent of the workday (Colwell, 2015). The fact that, for many leaders, this goal is seldom met on a daily basis only underscores the degree to which leaders can become bogged down in Tier 1 management activity at the expense of Tier 2 expert power activity and Tier 3 interpersonal skill activity. A thorough discussion of the concept of 50 percent leadership allocation on Tier 2 instructional leadership activity and Tier 3 interpersonal leadership activity will be discussed in chapter 5, "Getting to 50 Percent Tier 2 and 3 Behavior."

Chapter Three

The Leader as Instructional Expert (Tier 2)

As discussed in chapter 2, high-performing leaders need to be effective managers. Schools that are not run in a safe and orderly manner have very little hope of providing the kind of environment that teachers need in order to teach effectively and students need in order to learn effectively. Ensuring the safety of all students and stakeholders and ensuring that the overall environment and climate of the school allow for effective teaching and learning to take place are compelling conditions that every leader must achieve (Noonan, J., 2004).

In addition, schools that are not run efficiently have very little hope of managing the limited financial and human resources that are available to most school and district leaders. Any organization that is functioning with limited resources—and schools and school districts today certainly meet this description—must have leaders that understand how to manage those resources effectively.

The school systems of today were designed more than one hundred years ago, with an emphasis on efficiency and consistency. Our schools were designed to be able to mass-produce an educated population that could support the booming manufacturing economy that dominated the first eighty years of the twentieth century. As a result, the leader as a high-performing manager dominated the field of leader preparation and practitioner evaluation.

With the limited resources available to most education leaders, and with the multiple demands on school leaders' time, management activities still dominate much of the workday for education leaders. An honest evaluation of how leaders spend the workday—for instance, what tasks are occurring and what goals are being worked on—will show that managing the complex systems that are in operation for a school is often a time-consuming task.

When unforeseen events or "emergencies" are added to the leader's daily schedule, the combination of putting out fires and ensuring that all systems are running smoothly can easily dominate any school or district leader's calendar.

As a result of the need to educate workers for a manufacturing economy that was in place for much of the last century, the ability to lead a well-organized and efficient school that provided access to learning for students was sufficient at that time. The primary cultural and social battleground issues regarding education were not about the overall quality of the education being provided to students, but about the ability for all American citizens—regardless of race, gender, socioeconomic status, or disability—to participate in the system at all. Issues of equity and access dominated the public education landscape during most of the last century.

ACCESS TO SCHOOL FOR ALL

As the twentieth century dawned, many school systems enforced segregation for students of color, limited course offerings and opportunities for female students, and demonstrated a real lack of commitment or expertise in working toward providing a quality education of any type to immigrants or to children with disabilities. Many advocates for educational equality and opportunity dedicated their lives to the cause of a just and equitable American school system. During these decades, there was a struggle to realize the fundamental assumption that all children should have the right to attend school and receive a good education. Once that right was attained, advocates believed, all would be well.

The education battles of the time centered not on the quality of a school, but on the right to be able to attend school. The right to access school implied the student would get a quality education if they could simply attend. In this environment, the leader's role was to provide that assumed quality education in a safe, secure, efficient, and consistent way. The leader as a high-performing manager was therefore seen as sufficient for this purpose.

ACCESS TO QUALITY FOR ALL

The transition from a national focus on ensuring access to education for all children, to the more recent focus on the quality of education that all children were receiving once they had access to school, began in the late 1950s and accelerated over the next three decades following a series of events that brought into question the role and quality of our nation's schools, and with it, the role and responsibilities of our nation's school leaders.

Events such as the launch of the Russian spy satellite *Sputnik* in the late 1950s raised serious questions about the quality of our nation's curriculum. Policymakers wondered whether our children were receiving the necessary rigor in the areas of math and science to be able to compete in this new scientific age with the communist bloc nations. Why was America losing the space race? Were our schools to blame? Was the current child-centered emphasis of Dewey's progressive education movement actually beneficial? Were our schools actually producing graduates capable of competing on the world stage?

During the middle of the twentieth century, progressive, child-centered education was focused on experiential learning. Its goal was to develop the ability of students to problem-solve and to think critically. *Sputnik* caused policymakers to question the education philosophy in place in schools, as well as the rigor of the nation's curriculum. Was the Progressive Movement championed by educators such as John Dewey serving the national interest when it came to preparing school graduates to be productive workers in the fields that mattered to policymakers? Were the "essential" skills needed to be competitive in areas such as mathematics and science being taught often enough and with enough rigor?

At this time, primary changes to education came in the form of curricular reform. More teacher training in the areas of mathematics and the sciences was instituted. In addition, more teacher control of the curriculum was given to ensure that all children received more time in STEM fields and that those subjects were designed to be more rigorous and competitive on the world stage.

The rise of Japan as an economic superpower in the 1970s only reinforced the questions and concerns regarding the ability of America's school system to produce highly skilled workers who could compete in an international economy. Why was a foreign power able to outproduce, in both volume and product quality, the American worker when it came to automobiles or other "high-tech" consumer products?

These questions about school quality and graduate outcomes continued the transition away from a focus on access to schooling as a cultural imperative and moved it toward a focus on a higher quality of schooling as a cultural imperative. Questions regarding not only the quality of the curricula, but the quality, and accountability, of the educators themselves, were beginning to be asked. These questions led many to ask perhaps the most damning question of all: Are our school leaders and schoolteachers to blame for this economic threat?

Finally, the harshly critical report on the quality of American public education, *A Nation at Risk*, released in the 1980s, further challenged the status quo of school quality and school leadership. Perhaps in the history of the country there has never been a more damaging, and widely reported, document disseminated to the public than *A Nation at Risk*, with such damning statements as, "If a foreign power had done to America's children what our schools are doing to America's children, we would consider it an act of war" (*A Nation at Risk*, 1983).

The very notion that America's schools were waging war on America's children through a ubiquitous lack of quality and accountability still resonates in many sectors of society forty years later. The movement to centralize curricula and decision-making away from the teacher and the school leader and move it out to state and federal government control began to occur. The modern Standards Movement was, in many ways, born out of the hysteria generated by *A Nation at Risk* (Hunt, W.H., 2008).

The movement toward standards-based instruction and standardized testing, as a means to ensure that subject matter content had been taught and retained by students, took hold and has continued to accelerate for nearly thirty years. No longer was the word of the teacher that the student had mastered the subject matter good enough. Independent accountability would determine the extent to which students were academically prepared.

The belief by many policymakers that the modern school system, now fundamentally accessible to all children, was no longer, or perhaps never had been, a quality system in the first place has had obvious far-reaching consequences and impact on the twenty-first-century school. From an emphasis on standardized testing to ensure student learning, to increasing demands on teacher training and job performance, almost every aspect of America's schools over the last thirty years has been subject to increasing criticism, accountability, and calls for reform.

THE INSTRUCTIONAL LEADER

The type of leader needed to reform or transform this new generation of schools was seen as someone who needed much more than the managerial skills required in the early twentieth century. Policymakers questioned what good it was doing the country if a school was well managed, and was safe and orderly, if rigorous learning outcomes were not being achieved.

Legislatures across America began implementing, along with the support of educational associations, mandates that school leaders be trained in, and effective at, instructional leadership (DuFour, 2002). What good was it to have an efficient school system if students did not graduate, or if students graduated but could not demonstrate the fundamental skills needed for the modern workforce?

It appeared clear that, in addition to leaders with great management skills, leaders with expert skills in the fields of teaching, learning, and accountability were also needed. The recognition that leaders as highly skilled managers only would not suffice for the new modern school system, which needed to emerge as a result of economic pressures and global competition, has dominated leadership training in the education field for many decades. These societal pressures, and a focus on the leader as technical expert, that is, an expert in the field of teaching and learning, remain in place today. The *instructional leader* is the second tier of leadership skills and effectiveness.

As a result, a new, additional set of skills would be needed of the school leader. This new set of leadership skills would require school leaders to have technical expertise. This technical skill set involved the ability of the leader to have "expert" power in the field of teaching and learning, to be an "instructional leader," to be a "teacher of teachers" and an evaluator of teaching effectiveness.

For much of the last few decades of the twentieth century, and continuing into the first two decades of the twenty-first century, the notion of the high-performing leader as a management expert *and* as an instructional expert has dominated our view of what great leadership in school systems should look like. This expectation has guided our graduate schools of education and our infield professional development for new and veteran school leaders for the last forty years.

In an environment in which the overall quality of the education being provided is in question, a school leader who is not well versed in pedagogy, instructional frameworks, formative and summative assessment, curriculum, teacher evaluation, program accountability, and professional-development best practices, to name just a few areas of technical expertise needed to understand what good schools with effective teaching and meaningful learning look like, is doomed to failure regardless of the level of the leader's management expertise.

In this standardized academic view of the purpose of schooling in America, the modern education leader must understand what it means to be in the education business, that is, what the primary purpose of school is. A backlash against progressive education that began in the 1940s replaced a teacher- and child-centered curricula with a more "essential" curricula designed at the state and national level with input from business and civic leaders.

Schools were not day-care centers designed merely to house students while parents were at work. Schools were not places where the children decided what it was they wanted to learn or how they wanted to spend their time. The arts and the humanities were considered "soft" subjects that did not support the national interests in an era of world economic markets and competition. Teaching and learning a new modern, rigorous curricula, and ensuring that this teaching was done with quality and that the learning was truly mastered by all students, was at the very core of the school mission and was to comprise the majority of the daily activities of the instructional leader.

Even though leadership training and leadership expectations had shifted at that point from the leader as manager to the leader as instructional leader, far too often, management issues, such as student discipline and safety, facilities issues, master schedules, district and state level paperwork completion, and so forth still made up the majority of many leaders' days.

Today it is widely recognized that the leaders of a school or a school system should have expert power in the many areas that make up the best practices associated with teaching and learning. It makes sense for the leader to be an expert in the business in which he or she is leading. Every profession has a set of technical skills, a knowledge base, a profession-specific vocabulary, and metrics that must be understood and evaluated for success.

It would never be reasonable to assume that the leader of a large airport could be high performing while knowing little or nothing about air transportation and all of the systems that make up a high-quality airport. Who would want to be in a hospital where the CEO did not have a strong understanding of the medical sector and the technical and people skills needed to lead all of the employees in that hospital effectively toward the hospital's common mission?

What does success look like for an airport or a hospital leader? What training and support do airport workers or hospital workers need in order to be highly productive? What should be measured and evaluated, and what standards in the profession (sector) are considered "best practice"? The answers to all of these questions, and many more, rely on the technical expertise and skill sets associated with that particular profession. The skills, the expertise, associated with the specific mission of any organization, including education, are the Tier 2 leadership skills necessary for high-impact leadership.

The leader who can manage an airport (Tier 1), but who doesn't know what a high-performing, or a low-performing, airport looks like, or how to improve it, is doomed to be ineffective at best, and dangerous at worst. The same is true for the manager of the hospital or the leader of any profession who is skilled in areas associated with management, but who is not skilled at the technical knowledge (Tier 2) associated with that particular organization.

The same is true for the education sector. Simply put, education leaders who do not have technical expertise in the field of teaching and learning cannot lead educational institutions successfully, no matter how skilled they are at school management.

In educational leadership, these Tier 2 skills are often referred to as teaching and learning skills, or expert power skills. School board members, superintendents, teachers, and parents all are looking for, and expect, their school leaders to be instructional leaders, to have this expert power.

It is expected that these instructional leaders will take advantage of that expertise to move the organization forward by analyzing the current state of teaching and learning in the school or district, and then implementing development activities and other strategies designed to increase the quality of teaching and learning. It is expected that the school leader will take responsibility for ensuring that learning is occurring and that the leader is committed to spending the time needed to reach that primary goal. It is expected that the leader as expert will also hold everyone involved in the organization accountable to the standards of the profession, including pedagogical best practices.

It is considered a compliment of high praise when stakeholders and colleagues describe a principal or a superintendent as an "instructional leader," signifying that he or she possesses an important skill set that goes well beyond the leader as a high-performing manager. In fact, it would be considered damning with faint praise to say of a school leader, that he or she is "such a great manager of our school." The belief from parents, teachers, and all stakeholders that the school leader should have expert power in the field of teaching and learning is not only very important to the leader; it is, in fact, a prerequisite for success.

That belief by all stakeholders that the leader is an expert allows the leader to be seen as having the skills and credibility to do the job well. It gives the leader credibility with teachers, and it gives the leader confidence from parents and students. Because of the importance placed on the technical skill of being an instructional leader, most graduate educational leadership programs spend a great deal of time training and assessing each candidate's ability to serve as an instructional expert. Most school districts hiring new leaders focus extensively on their candidate pool to ensure that the leaders they are selecting have pedagogical expertise.

When combined with the leader's ability to also manage the organization effectively, these two tiers—the leader as high-performing manager, and the leader as instructional expert—comprise the vast majority of what leaders are trained to be and how leaders are assessed.

Even when education leaders develop the skill sets and behaviors necessary to both manage and serve as instructional leaders well, however, there is a third tier of leadership expertise and skill needed. In today's educational environment, the ability to be a high-performing manager and a high-performing expert in the field of teaching and learning, while still necessary, is not sufficient.

The modern education leader must also be an interpersonal expert. Team-building skills; the ability to articulate and lead mission-driven activity; and the ability to excel in the "soft skills" of interpersonal relationship building, conflict resolution, and goal setting—these all must also be mastered by school leaders at every level. This third tier of leadership, the leader as interpersonal expert, is introduced in chapter 4, and the skills and dispositions necessary to achieve this Tier 3 leadership are discussed in depth in section 2.

Chapter Four

The Leader as Interpersonal Expert (Tier 3)

As discussed in earlier chapters, today's school leaders must be outstanding managers of school and district operations, as well as instructional experts, fluent in pedagogical best practice. Management power and expert power make up the first two tiers of the impactful leader. While these two leadership tiers are necessary, they are not, in and of themselves, sufficient to truly lead with impact in the twenty-first century.

A third, emerging level of leadership skill focuses on the ability of the leader to build upon, and enhance, the complex interpersonal relationships that exist within any school organization. These attributes, skills, and leadership aspirations allow the leader to focus on what Peter Senge calls the "fundamental learning unit" of any high-performing organization: the team (Senge, P.M., 2006).

The "soft skills" needed to build large teams working toward a common mission, the communication skills needed to articulate complex solutions to complex problems, and the ability to motivate, influence, and inspire colleagues and stakeholders to achieve at the highest levels require a set of skills and behaviors that are distinct from the skills needed to manage the organization effectively or the skills needed to have an expert level of understanding regarding how teaching and learning work.

WHY SHOULD ANYONE BE LED BY YOU?

How leaders perceive themselves, as managers, or as experts, or as team builders, will determine how they answer a simple, but seldom-asked question: Why should anyone be led by you? This is an essential question that all school leaders should ponder.

Many leaders take for granted that by virtue of being in a leadership position, with the power and the authority to lead the organization that is granted by their job description, followers will follow, all stakeholders will comply with leadership directives, and the leader's agenda will simply be promoted, because that is how the organization is structured. As a result, this question is seldom asked, and seldom contemplated by most leaders, but the ability to answer the question in a clear and believable way is critical to the leadership mind-set of the Tier 3 leader.

It is easy for anyone in a formal leadership position, with all of their job prerequisites met, with the job description outlined, and with the power of the position bestowed, to assume that the answer to this question is simple. It is easy to simply assume that the answer is because the leader has been assigned the leadership role by those in a position to make that assignment.

When the answer to the question "Why should anyone be led by me" is "Because it is my job to lead," that leader is operating from a Tier 1 (leader as manager) mind-set. Built upon a bureaucratic structure with clear lines of authority, the Tier 1 leader rarely even contemplates the question, because the answer is usually self-evident. The leader should be followed because the leader's job description places the leader in a position of line authority.

Tier 2 leaders, who place great value on the power of knowledge and expertise, answer the question in a different way. The Tier 2 leader does not expect colleagues to follow based on his or her position title, but on the demonstrated proof that the holder of the position is a proven expert in the field of teaching and learning; in short, because he or she is an instructional leader.

Concerning the ability to demonstrate a command of the subject at hand, whether it is pedagogical best practice, learning theory, motivation theory, or instructional frameworks and design, the fact that the leader has proven expertise in these technical areas and more should be enough for all stakeholders to follow.

The Tier 2 leader assumes that expert power is the answer to the question. And once expert power is demonstrated on a continuous basis, the leader believes that he or she will have the support and commitment from the stakeholders in the organization.

Tier 3 leaders view the answer to the question "Why should anyone be led by you?" from a third, and different, perspective. Like Tier 2 leaders, who value expert power above all else, Tier 3 leaders see leadership as earned, not given. The difference centers upon what type of expertise the leader values most. Tier 3 leaders see leadership as a collective enterprise built around the ability of the leader to be team oriented and mission driven. Tier 3 leaders recognize that teams can only function effectively in climates in which interpersonal relationships are built upon trust (Gillespie & Mann, 2004). Trust in all of the leaders—trust in the team itself—forms the foundation for Tier 3 leadership.

In this context, leadership is not seen as having technical knowledge about the subject at hand, which is often the providence of an exceptional few, but it is seen as a set of behaviors and skills that can be accessed by anyone in the organization (Kouzes and Posner, 2010). Tier 3 leaders value distributed leadership. Tier 3 leaders recognize the fundamental importance of building powerful teams working toward a common mission.

Tier 3 leaders recognize that powerful and meaningful missions motivate, influence, and provide job satisfaction to employees (Perry & Hondeghem, 2008). Tier 3 leaders believe that followers are also part of the leadership team, and that what is really being "followed" is not any one leader, but a common mission that has significant worth.

LEADERS AS TEAM BUILDERS

The leader as a builder of teams is a critical component of the Tier 3 leadership mind-set. The leader who is committed to building a team of leaders recognizes that no one individual can solve the complex issues associated with educating today's students. No one individual, or even the entire administrative team, can effectively manage the complex environment of today's large and diverse schools, with the multitude of stakeholder obligations and local, state, and national regulations that must be effectively addressed on a daily basis. No individual or small group of leaders have all of the expertise, knowledge, and wisdom necessary to achieve all of the organization's goals.

Knowing that schools must be managed efficiently, a time-consuming process, and knowing that a great deal of technical expertise on a wide range of subjects must exist within the leadership framework, the Tier 3 leader recognizes a simple fact: There is *no one individual* who possesses all of the strengths and qualities necessary to accomplish all three levels of leadership skills simultaneously. Even if this mythical "super leader" did exist, there is nowhere near enough time for that leader to accomplish and attend to all of the Tier 1, Tier 2, and Tier 3 tasks on a daily basis.

There is more, however, to the Tier 3 leadership mind-set than recognizing that no single individual, no matter how skilled or dedicated, has the ability to lead a school alone. Leaders who are committed to meaningful and powerful collaboration recognize that the "smartest person in the room is the room" (Weinberger, 2014).

Leadership capacity grows when the number of "leaders" in the room grows. Leadership is seen as a team sport, not just because the job is too complex for any one individual to accomplish, but because Tier 3 leaders recognize that the team is always going to be more impactful and successful together than any one member of the team will be in isolation, no matter how skilled or credentialed that one team member might be.

High-impact Tier 3 leaders spend significant time building and nurturing teams of educators, because they recognize that what gets accomplished will always be impacted by the work of others (Botha, 2004). High-impact leaders delegate both authority and responsibility to these teams, so that they may play a major role not just in supporting organizational-management activity, but also mission-driven activity. These teams are assigned to accomplish powerful, impactful organizational objectives.

Tier 3 leaders recognize that this requires much more than the delegation of routine tasks or the delegation of tasks without the authority to accomplish those tasks. Tier 3 leaders don't just build, develop, and empower teams; they empower teams on a mission.

LEADERS AS MISSION BUILDERS

Tier 3 leadership requires more than just developing strategies that lead to the development of teams of leaders. It is not enough for teams to simply exist; they must also be empowered and inspired by a meaningful mission. It is the mission that matters, and the leader who is able to motivate, to collaborate, and to compel the organization's stakeholders to action is the leader who will succeed in accomplishing the mission (Goleman, Boyatzis, & McKee, 2013).

This concept of the meaningful mission is another key component in the Tier 3 leadership mind-set. In this context, the "meaningful mission" has very specific attributes. These attributes are different from the typical list of tasks and objectives to be accomplished that are routinely assigned by the school or district leader to others to accomplish so that the leader can spend time on more "important" issues.

Within any given school day, week, or year, there are literally hundreds of tasks that leaders and leadership teams need to accomplish. These tasks are important. They need to be done correctly, on time, and efficiently. If these tasks are not accomplished, or if they are mismanaged in some way, there are real consequences to the functioning of the organization.

Think of any sector within a school. Transportation, food service, the master schedule, extracurricular activities, and the testing calendar are just a few of a wide range of job responsibilities that require specific action and oversight. These missions are obviously important. The ability for the organization to function as a well-managed operation (Tier 1), and the ability for the organization to focus on teaching and learning (Tier 2), are both built upon the ability of the organization to manage these important tasks effectively. While these tasks are important to the leader and all stakeholders, they are not, in and of themselves, meaningful to the organization's stakeholders.

There is a difference between an important task and a meaningful mission. It is important that the lunchroom functions smoothly, that the food is properly prepared and served, that the schedule for feeding all of the students operates smoothly, that the lunchroom is a safe and welcoming environment for all students. All of these tasks, these goals, are important. Whether it is food service, transportation services, financial services, or managing the master schedule, the need for a well-managed and successful outcome for each sector of the organization is clear.

Missions with meaning, however, require something more than just being important to the smooth operation of the school. In fact, what makes the types of goals described above important is that the successful implementation of these Tier 1 tasks is what allows the members of the organization to pursue their primary mission.

Tier 3 leaders want the lunchroom, the master schedule, and the school budget to run smoothly *so that all stakeholders can focus on what really matters to the organization*. These management tasks are prerequisites for the primary mission of the organization. These Tier 1 tasks must be successful so that the primary mission of the school can occur. Tier 3 leaders recognize that the primary mission of the school is to make a difference in the lives of the students they serve. Tier 3 leaders recognize that it is the power and scope of this mission that truly motivates and inspires all stakeholders.

In this context, it is the primary goal of Tier 3 leadership to articulate that meaningful mission to the leadership team and all stakeholders using a powerful set of interpersonal skills. It is a recognition that the ability to define the big mission, and to grow, develop, influence, and motivate the leadership team and all stakeholders to work toward that mission on a daily basis, is what separates Tier 3 leadership from Tier 1 and Tier 2 leadership.

DEVELOPMENT OF SELF-EFFICACY

High-performing leaders all have a strong commitment to the organization's primary mission. This focus on the big picture, on the mission that matters most and the use of a "mission voice" to lead and motivate stakeholders to be the best they can be on behalf of the mission, is critical.

Leaders also, however, need to have a strong sense of belief in themselves and their own ability to meet the demands and responsibilities of leadership. Why should anyone follow a leader who does not believe in themself? How can leaders influence and motivate followers to reach their potential, even when that potential seems out of reach, if they do not see that same potential for excellence in themselves?

In addition to being highly skilled in management, in technical expertise, and in people skills, leaders also need to be able to develop and believe in their own self-efficacy. In this context, *self-efficacy* is a "leader's belief in their ability to exercise control and command over their own level of functioning and over all of the events that will impact each day's work and relationships" (Bandura, 1993). The ability to believe in oneself is critical to success and impact at all levels of the organization.

Research by Gibson and Dembo (1984) and by Goddard, Hoy, and Woolfolk (2000) on the relationship between teacher impact and teacher self-efficacy shows clear correlations between the degrees to which teachers demonstrate self-efficacy and the quality of work produced. Educators at all levels within the organization with high levels of confidence set high goals for themselves, are persistent in their work, and do not give up when faced with setbacks or adversity. In addition, these educators are more open to trying new and innovative approaches in order to meet the organization's goals.

The same is true for leaders in the organization. It is the combination of the belief in the value of the mission, and the belief in the ability to not only accomplish that mission, but also to be one of the leaders who ensures that the mission is accomplished, that has true impact. Leaders who believe in the mission but not in themselves will not succeed. Similarly, leaders who believe in themselves but not in the value of the mission, or who do not understand what the mission even is, may be able to lead a well-managed school, but they are highly unlikely to succeed at leading the organization toward the powerful goal of making a significant difference in the lives of the students in the organization.

And so, the fundamental leadership question remains: Why should anyone be led by you? The simple answer is, because you are team driven and primary mission oriented. The answer is, because the teams that you seek to build and empower are given the responsibility, the authority, and the resources to lead meaningful missions. The answer is, because the mission that you communicate and support, in word and in deed, has real meaning and significance, not only to the lives of the students, but also to the lives of the teachers, the staff, and the administrators—to all stakeholders.

While the answer to the question may seem simple, the ability to deliver the mission successfully and consistently to all stakeholders is complex, daunting, and requires a set of daily leadership skills. These Tier 3 leadership attributes and the daily strategies that Tier 3 leaders use to accomplish the mission are discussed further in section 2.

The knowledge, skills, and attributes necessary to be an impactful leader in the complex and ever-changing world of education in the twenty-first century are still evolving. The school leader with management skills would have been considered well equipped to lead the schools of the early twentieth century. The leader with management skills, as well as considerable expertise in the art and science of learning, what is often called the instructional leader, would be considered high performing and fully prepared to lead a school or a school district until just a few years ago.

Universities preparing new school leaders and district professional development programs for sitting school and district leaders spend significant amounts of time and energy training and developing the management (efficiency) skills and the technical (teaching and learning best practice) skills of school leaders.

While the ability for leaders to have these skills is critical for the success of the school leader and the organizations they serve, the leader who can only lead through management and instructional skill will not succeed in leading today's schools to their fullest potential. In the volatile world that is P–12 education today, that leader is missing a third, and most important, set of leadership skills: the ability to lead as an interpersonal expert. The ability to lead with the "soft skills" that are often described as "people skills" or "interpersonal skills" is the critical leadership competency for the high-impact twenty-first-century school leader. Put simply, an education leader without people skills will never be exceptional.

The Tier 3 leader is more than an efficient organizational manager, more than an expert in the technical frameworks that describe best practices in the field. The Tier 3 leader is an expert team builder, mission definer, and motivator. The Tier 3 leader knows how to build powerful cultures centered on profound organizational missions, and he or she recognizes that above all else, this is the most important and impactful attribute the modern education leader can possess.

For the Tier 3 leader, it is the mission that matters. To be more precise, it is the big mission that matters, the mission that actually empowers all educators with the skills, the ability, the inspiration, and the authority to impact the lives of all students in ways that go well beyond any test score.

For this team-oriented, mission-driven structure to work, the overall climate and culture of the organization becomes the top priority of the Tier 3 leader (Kelley, Thornton, & Daugherty, 2005). The values of open communication, team-oriented work, and distribution of power and decision-making authority become the highest daily priorities for the Tier 3 leader.

Position power is of no real use to the leader in this context, other than to ensure that everyone in the organization is both physically and emotionally safe and to ensure that all aspects of the organization, and everyone involved in the organization, operate in legal and ethical ways. Aside from those priorities, where the Tier 3 leader does not hesitate to use position power if needed, the only leadership skills that really matter to the leader are those skills that culminate in empowered teams on an audacious mission.

Simply put, the school or district leader who understands how to run an efficient organization and understands the complexities and attributes that make up successful teaching and learning, but who cannot or will not use the skills necessary for building distributed leadership teams authorized to lead meaningful mission activities, will fail. Leaders who place the highest value and priority on building and growing teams of leaders who are motivated and inspired to make a difference in the lives of the students they serve, are likely to succeed.

Chapter Five

Get to 50 Percent Tier 2 and Tier 3 Behavior

In chapter 4, a fundamental question was addressed: Why should anyone be led by you? The recognition that leaders are worth following not because of their management skills and their technical teaching and learning skills, but because of their orientation to a team-centered approach to decision-making and their ability to articulate and follow, in word and deed, a mission-driven culture is an important prerequisite to Tier 3 Behavior #1: Getting to 50 Percent Tier 2 and Tier 3 Behavior (Colwell, 2015).

Why should anyone follow a leader? Because that leader spends the majority of their time on Tier 2 teaching and learning activities and on Tier 3 interpersonal human capacity–development leadership activities.

In complex environments such as schools, where management and operational activities can easily dominate a leader's day, many leaders become firefighters, responding to one event or crisis after another. The leader's day becomes a series of ad-hoc meetings, reactive decision-making situations, and the management of a multitude of operational and short-term problem-solving events.

Leaders who take the time to track their daily activities and sort those activities into management-related and non-management-related activities are often shocked to see how much time has been spent during the day dealing with organizational operations and management. The simple truth is that how leaders actually spend their time matters and is often not understood (Ammons & Newell, 1989). How much time a leader is spending on any of the myriad job responsibilities and functions will go a long way in describing what that leader values.

While important, and certainly time-consuming, these management-related activities should not be seen as containing significant elements of meaningful interpersonal skill leadership, as management activity does not build vision and does not support direction-setting activities for the organization (Kotte, 2008). Operational goals should support the overall mission of the organization; they are not, however, of equal importance nor do they have equal impact on the organization. The primary reason to have the busses run on time is so that students can be in school and learn. The primary reason to have a safe and orderly campus is so that students can learn in an environment of respect.

It is not the mission of the school to be a well-managed environment. Well-managed environments are prerequisites for the school's mission, not the mission itself. It should be the mission of the school to make a difference in the lives of the students. It should be the mission of the school to ensure that every student is educated and able to use that education to choose whatever life path that is desired after graduation.

Whether the student wishes to pursue further education, enter the workforce directly, or enter into some type of military or community service, it is the school's responsibility to provide the education necessary to ensure that outcome. Managing the school may be a prerequisite for meeting these challenging goals successfully, but it is not, in and of itself, an indicator of organizational success.

THE TIER 1 TRAP

It is easy for today's school leaders to find themselves trapped conducting management activities. As a first-year assistant principal recently wrote in response to a training session on building leadership capacity, "I have been spending so much time dealing with all the different procedural issues of being in administration, I was not focusing on the one reason I started my career in education, the student. I have been spending all my time on the functioning of the office and realized that if I had to choose to cut something out, it would be the time in the classroom. When I plotted my time, I found out that 67 percent of my day was being spent on managing" (Churms, 2016).

It is not at all uncommon for any school leader to be trapped in Tier 1 leadership activities. The management trap is not the sole province of the assistant principal or the beginning administrator. Any leader at any level of the organization and at any level of experience within the organization is highly susceptible to becoming trapped as a Tier 1 leader.

Every leader's day is extremely busy with a multitude of job responsibilities, meetings, reports, and decisions to be made. Often the leader will not even be aware that the majority of the workday is being spent on managing the daily operations of the school as opposed to spending significant time on instructional or interpersonal leadership to build and support the culture and mission of the school. It is easy for the leader to assume that the way the day is being spent, the way time is being allocated, and the tasks that are being given the highest priority are exactly what the job calls for.

It is also easy to assume that all other leaders in similar positions are spending their workdays the same way. It is easy to push off the "softer" leadership demands of mission building, trust building, and teamwork for another day. Management activities often come with hard deadlines; reports are due on a specific date. Phone calls and e-mails all seem urgent and time sensitive. It is a common practice for the leader to believe that little harm will come to the school if the leader doesn't get to focus on teaching and learning on a certain day. There is always tomorrow for that.

The first step, then, for any leader who wants to spend at least 50 percent of their work time on Tier 2 and Tier 3 behaviors is to understand how the typical workday is actually being spent. Leaders cannot change their behavior if they don't understand what their current behavior actually is. While the steps and suggestions discussed here may seem simple to complete, they do require a commitment of time and consistency of action. In this case, the leader must take the time to understand current daily leadership behavior in order to make the time to initiate new practices.

WHY 50 PERCENT?

Why should leaders adapt behaviors that ensure that at least 50 percent of their workdays are spent on Tier 2 and Tier 3 leadership behavior? Shouldn't the leader spend more than that percentage of their time on these critical leadership activities? Wouldn't 60 percent, 75 percent, or 90 percent be a more appropriate daily goal? This author admits that the goal of spending a minimum of 50 percent of each day on activities clearly associated with improving the quality of teaching and learning and/or the quality of the communication, culture, and climate of the school is based on an arbitrary number, but it is a number grounded in a recognition of the reality of the constraints that face today's school leaders.

After tracking daily leadership behavior for many leaders over hundreds of days, in environments ranging from elementary school to high school to large district offices, it has become clear that most leaders today are unfortunately nowhere near spending 50 percent of their work time on activities and behaviors associated with either Tier 2 teaching and learning activities or Tier 3 interpersonal skill development behaviors.

The example from the year-one assistant principal, trapped in Tier 1 management behavior, is very typical. Her daily tracking of actual behaviors and tasks identified only 33 percent of the workday being allocated to Tier 2 and Tier 3 behaviors. Why target 50 percent as the daily goal? Because most leaders currently spend significantly less than 50 percent of their time on Tier 2 and Tier 3 behaviors. For most school leaders, 50 percent is a stretch goal.

There are, however, specific strategies that leaders can use to limit the amount of the workday that is dedicated to managerial and/or technical activities to no more than 50 percent. These strategies help the leader get to 50 percent of the workday being dedicated to teaching, learning, and mission-building activity.

This is the 50 Percent Rule: As a leader, spend a minimum of 50 percent of each workday dedicated to Tier 2 instructional leadership activities and Tier 3 interpersonal skill leadership activities. In order to "Get to 50 Percent," the leader must first know the difference between management activities and leadership activities. Second, the leader must prioritize leadership time on the calendar as higher, or at least as high, in importance as management time (Colwell, 2015).

KNOW WHAT YOU ARE DOING

School and district leaders are, without question, busy professionals. Anyone who has shadowed a school leader for a day will see hundreds of human interactions involving scores of issues, big and small. The leader's day is packed with meetings, phone calls, reports, urgent events, and other obligations, all of which are time consuming.

It is not an exaggeration to say that every educational leader can easily fill up the workday and beyond with managing the daily operation of the school or district. The question that busy educational leaders face is not whether there are important activities and issues that need to be addressed today, but how those multitude of issues should be prioritized and integrated into the day's schedule of activities.

Often the hectic pace of the day and the wide variety of activities that occur during the day can leave the leader unsure of how the day was actually spent. When this happens, the leader knows that he or she was very busy, but is just not sure where the day went or what was actually accomplished.

For leaders who are spending a great deal of each day reacting to unfolding events, the first step in getting to 50 percent daily Tier 2 and Tier 3 activity is to really know how their current workday is being spent. How much of the leader's day, day in and day out, is spent on the management of the school or the district? If the leader doesn't know what percent of their time is consumed with management activity, the leader cannot consciously change their behavior in order to allocate more time for Tier 2 and Tier 3 behaviors.

The simplest way to track daily behavior is to log daily behavior. Keeping an accurate log of the day's activities and how much time was spent on each activity takes time and discipline. It can be easy to dismiss the need to keep a log, believing that understanding the day's activities is already clear and a record is not needed. In this view, the leader believes he or she can keep mental track of what is occurring each day and how much time these activities are taking. That is a mistake.

It is also easy to postpone the few minutes needed at the end of the day to record the day's activities, because if there is not enough time to do what is already on the list, keeping a log of the day becomes just one more activity for which there is no time. Delaying this activity or moving the activity to a weekly event rather than a daily event is also a mistake. To truly understand how time is being allocated, a clear and accurate record, maintained over a period of days and weeks, is needed. On any given day, or even on any given week, serious management issues will consume the time of any leader, no matter how committed to instructional and interpersonal leadership behavior that leader is.

Conversely, any leader will experience days or weeks in which the calendar is friendly to Tier 2 and Tier 3 behaviors. Over time, however, the dominant use of leadership time will always emerge. Knowing how leadership time is currently being spent is the critical first step to changing how leadership time is going to be spent. Impactful leaders log their activities over time on a consistent basis.

KNOW WHY YOU ARE DOING

Changing leadership behavior to prioritize daily activity focused on instructional leadership and interpersonal leadership will require the understanding and cooperation of many stakeholders. Moving routine daily management activity to the part of the day in which instruction is not occurring and in which stakeholders are not formally engaged with the school means that the leader will need to complete those activities later in the day, or perhaps even early the next morning. Responses to non-emergency management and daily operation issues that might have occurred within minutes may now not occur for several hours.

Keep in mind that not every management issue is an *emergency* management issue. Responses that might have always been handled directly by a particular leader may be widely distributed to members of a management team. Building teams and providing those teams with the capacity and authority to complete management tasks is a Tier 3 behavior that will immediately reduce the leader's need to always be directly involved in Tier 1 behaviors.

Teachers, students, parents, and other stakeholders will likely want to know why the leader is not now immediately available to return a phone call or meet with them in person. Stakeholders will want to know why someone other than the leader is responding to their concern or inquiry. Particularly when the leader's daily calendar has, until now, slotted school management activities as the highest priority, and particularly where the leader has a reputation for always being available and always prompt to return stakeholders' calls or respond to the e-mails gathering during the day, the ability to articulate the reasons behind changing the leader's daily activities to a focus on Tier 2 and Tier 3 behaviors is critical for success.

The good news for leaders working to increase their capacity to lead is that for teachers, parents, and stakeholders who are vested in the success of the school, what everyone wants as a top priority is the same: student success. When making a difference in the lives of students is the leader's top priority, and when that priority is clearly articulated by the leader, not only will internal and external stakeholders understand the daily priorities of the leader, they will also work to support those priorities. Stakeholder understanding of why the leader spends time in certain ways is critical to the success of the leader's efforts to get to 50 percent.

HONESTY IS THE BEST POLICY

Everyone, including high-performing leaders, can be guilty of rationalizing behavior. It is easy for leaders who are spending 60 or 70 percent of each day or more managing the multitude of complex issues and operations necessary to have a smoothly running school or district, to believe that they are spending that much time because no one else has the skill sets needed to do the tasks, or at least to do them as well as the leader. After all, the leader is ultimately responsible for every aspect of the organization.

It can also be easy for the leader to believe that every management issue is some form of emergency that requires intervention and action from the top of the organization. In this mind-set, leaders don't delegate issues that are of high priority, that are deemed "emergencies." If every event, however, is a high priority or an urgent event, then the leader is caught in a catch-22, unwilling to delegate responsibility and authority to others in the organization and thus trapped with insufficient time to be a proactive Tier 3 leader.

It is easy for leaders who are trying to keep track of their daily behavior to categorize management behavior as team-building behavior or teaching and learning behavior. When leaders spend time on routine managing tasks but believe that those tasks are actually building team capacity or interpersonal capacity, because the tasks are important and do involve many other members of the organization, the leader is inaccurately coding Tier 1 behaviors as Tier 2 or Tier 3 behaviors.

As with any set of data, the analysis of the data is dependent on the accuracy of the data. Logging activities with colleagues as team-building Tier 3 activity just because a group of individuals were involved in the meeting, when the entire purpose of the meeting was to reorganize the bus schedule (a Tier 1 activity) so that student tardiness is less likely, may increase the perceived amount of time spent getting to 50 percent, but it does not change the "facts on the ground" that the time was actually spent on a management issue.

This is not to say that the meeting was not needed, was not worthwhile, or did not require the presence of the leader. All of these caveats may be perfectly true. But it is also true that the meeting was a Tier 1 event. In order to clearly understand the use of leadership time, the leader must be willing to be brutally honest about recording accurately and coding accurately what happened during the day.

TIER 3 COMES FIRST

It is easy to see and understand the pressures of school management and the resulting tendency for daily operations to dominate the workday. School safety is job one. A safe and orderly school environment is a prerequisite for a learning school environment. For most stakeholders, how the school operates is all that is known about the school. For these stakeholders, a good school is a clean, quiet, and orderly school. It is also relatively easy to articulate the need for school leaders to increase the amount of time and attention spent on the primary mission of the school: teaching and learning.

The notion that the school leader is first and foremost an instructional leader has become deeply engrained in leadership dogma over the last forty years. Leaders who feel bogged down in firefighting the daily challenges and issues of the day recognize those activities and that time spent as coming at the expense of being in the classroom working with teachers and students. Most leaders will lament the lack of time available for classroom walk-throughs, for teacher support, for direct contact with students, and for strategic school-improvement planning.

It is not hard to get school leaders to buy in to the concept that Tier 2 instructional leadership should be a primary job responsibility. The same cannot be said for many leaders when it comes to truly recognizing the critical value of being a Tier 3 interpersonal skill leader and developer of others.

In order to get to 50 percent Tier 2 and Tier 3 behavior, it is not the need to understand the importance of instructional leadership that is critical to success; it is the need to understand the importance of getting to interpersonal skill leadership as a top priority for daily leadership activity (Mumford, Campion, & Morgeson, 2007). This is a harder concept for many school leaders to buy in to. The notion that time spent building and supporting interpersonal skills with all stakeholders is the most valuable use of the leader's time is not easily recognized for most leaders. In fact, for many educators, time spent on these perceived soft skills would be seen as the least productive use of time.

If the leader had to prioritize handling a daily operational issue, working on an issue that impacted teacher or student readiness, or working on developing relationships and building a team with a common mission, the mission-building activity would be deferred. The leadership irony is that it is the leader's team-building and mission-building activity that allows for meaningful instructional leadership activity to occur in the first place. It is the team-building and mission-building leadership activity that allows for the effective handling of management activity to be distributed to others.

In short, it is the ability to lead through strong interpersonal skills that allows the leader to use expert power as an instructional leader and position power as a manager of daily operations. It is the ability to lead through strong interpersonal skills that builds the capacity of others toward a powerful common mission that creates a team of leaders. As discussed earlier, in the volatile, uncertain, complex, and ambiguous environment that is the twenty-first-century school, it is not the leader that succeeds; it is the team of leaders that succeeds.

GET OUT

School and district leaders are used to following schedules. The good news is that with modern technology and a competent staff, the leader's calendar can easily be updated and maintained so that, at any time, the whereabouts of the leader is known. It is true that the school day is literally scheduled to the minute. When the first period will become the second period, when the fourth-grade lunch begins, when Bus 129 is scheduled to arrive—these are all examples of the many ways the environment in which the leader works is locked down. Even within the allotted instructional time of the school day, how much time is spent on reading or science or social studies is tracked to the minute.

One of the biggest challenges teachers face is the inability to control their own calendars. For teachers today, the ability to make decisions regarding how to best use their time has sadly been greatly diminished. Ironically, for leaders of schools and school districts, how time is used is still primarily under the control of the leader. For far too many leaders, the gift of controlling how time is spent, what activities are prioritized, and what activities are delegated to others or given to teams of leaders to accomplish are not thought out or controlled by the leaders. These leaders do not take advantage of the ability to control their own calendars.

The one aspect of the system that does not need to maintain a strict schedule is the leader's calendar itself, and yet by design or by omission, most leaders spend their days following a strict routine of firefighting and daily management operations. The school day is fixed; notwithstanding true emergencies, the time for lunch to begin and end is nonnegotiable. Only in the most extreme circumstances would a school leader change the bell schedule or the time at which the instructional school day ends and students head home.

Yet leaders too often let the events of the day guide the schedule rather than letting the leadership objectives of the day guide the schedule. Leaders who want to have an impact and be highly productive arrive at school with a specific set of goals and activities planned for the day. These planned activities prioritize a focus on the core missions of the school: making a difference for students and empowering the capacity of the adults in the building to teach. Important committee and stakeholder meetings are scheduled to build the capacity of the team and to improve the culture, climate, and communication within the school.

Within a few hours, however, or sometimes within a matter of minutes, the leader abandons the day's plotted-out schedule and priorities in order to deal with an unplanned event. Perhaps it is an angry parent with a real issue about a teacher or another student; perhaps it is an important stakeholder expecting a quick response to an area of concern that is important to that particular stakeholder and the represented group. Perhaps a student conduct issue has arisen, a substitute teacher has failed to arrive to cover a class, or someone from the district office or the state is asking for information.

The list of unplanned or unexpected events that can occur on any given day in a school or school district is too numerous to list. These events are ubiquitous. As a result, it is also common for the leader to spend too much of the instructional day on non-instructional Tier 1 activity.

This use of the day and how the leader responds to unplanned events often becomes a daily habit, a daily routine for the leader. First the leader plans for Tier 2 and Tier 3 activities to be accomplished during the day, then the leader encounters Tier 1 issues as described above, then the leader spends a great deal of the day (more than 50 percent) resolving those Tier 1 issues.

Once this happens enough, these routines become so engrained in the leader's daily behaviors, that the initial planning to be an instructional leader, to be an interpersonal leader who builds the capacity of others and serves to empower teams though expert power and mission-driven behaviors, is not even planned for by the leader anymore. Over time, the daily schedule for the leader simply absorbs the time needed to serve as a Tier 2/Tier 3 leader in order to manage the school. In the end, the leader, no matter how well intentioned, remains primarily a manager.

And yet the leader who has succumbed to these behaviors typically has built systems to handle the daily operations of the building when the leader is away at district or state meetings or is gone on that rare vacation. Too many leaders build systems that allow others to lead and manage the school or district while they are away, but then they immediately resume handling those Tier 1 duties when they return. Tier 3 leaders maintain teams of managers and teams of instructional leaders in order to diversify and distribute the multitude of routine management tasks that occur each and every day.

Tier 3 leaders also work to take control of their daily schedule by scheduling leadership time out of the office. Just as leaders take for granted that lunch occurs at a certain time, leaders can also build into the schedule time to be where instruction and stakeholders are as time certain. By taking the routine, but necessary leadership tasks that involve phone calls, e-mails, correspondence, and so forth, and moving those activities to those times of the day when teachers are not teaching and most stakeholders are not available, the leader can also build daily calendars that increase the probability of spending at least 50 percent of the day on Tier 2 and Tier 3 activities.

ALIGN ACTIVITIES WITH THE PHASES OF THE WORKDAY

It is a common practice for school and district leaders to begin each day with a review of e-mails received, phone calls that need to be returned, issues that have arisen from the previous day or the night before, a review of the calendar for the day, and due dates for short-term projects. The leadership trap associated with this orientation toward the day is not the need to understand the scope of the tasks at hand, but failing to prioritize, not only the order in which the tasks should be aligned in terms of importance, but also the order and the time of day in which they will be completed.

Getting to 50 percent requires the school leader to think about the workday as existing in three basic phases, each with its own unique purposes and opportunities. First, there is the part of the day in which teachers and students are present; this is the "instructional phase" of the school day. This is the part of the day that most stakeholders think of when they refer to the school day. The school day typically runs for six and one-half hours in most states for students, and approximately seven and one-half hours for teachers. It is during the instructional phase of the day that the opportunity to serve in the capacity of instructional leader is most available.

Second, there is the part of the day in which students, for the most part, are no longer on campus engaged in learning, but when teachers and other stakeholders are still actively engaged in the organization. After-school conferences and meetings are occurring, and extracurricular activities and after-school day-care programs are under way.

This phase of the day typically occurs just before and just after school, although when that second part of the day takes place varies from week to week depending on the stakeholders involved. On some days, days in which the Parent-Teacher Association, the band or athletic boosters, or any other number of formal stakeholder groups are meeting, phase two of the day could be right after school is let out for students; on other days, these phase two activities may take place in the early evening.

This is the "stakeholder part" of the day. The opportunity to work with internal and external stakeholders is high during this time period and throughout these activities. The ability to work collaboratively with colleagues and stakeholders, to establish important interpersonal relations, and to build, motivate, and influence the team are most likely to occur during this section of the day.

The third part of the leader's day involves that phase of the day in which student and stakeholder opportunities are no longer available, but when administrative responsibilities remain to be completed. Typically, this third phase of the day may not be during the day at all; it may be in the evening or very early in the morning before colleagues have arrived on campus. The opportunities to work in an uninterrupted way, on issues dealing with managing the daily operations of the school, are best served during this time period.

In order for any leader to get to 50 percent Tier 2 and Tier 3 leadership activity on a daily basis, the leader must match how he or she spends the day with the normal phases, the normal routines, of the day. If the leader is overinvolved in managerial work during phase 1 instructional time or phase 2 stakeholder time, the leader will not have any time to devote to stakeholder mission-building or instructional leadership-building activity. A sound strategy for managing the leader's calendar and the different natural phases of a typical school day is to try to move routine communication and management activity, such as e-mails and phone calls, to the end of the day or very early in the day.

By beginning the instructional day with colleagues, students, teachers, and stakeholders, rather than on the phone or performing routine management activities, the leader can increase the likelihood that 50 percent of the day will be directly connected to instructional and interpersonal leadership activity.

BE GOAL DRIVEN: EACH AND EVERY DAY THE TARGET IS 50 PERCENT

Even when all of the strategies discussed here are implemented, even when the leader has every intent to prioritize Tier 2 and Tier 3 behaviors, for most leaders on most days, the ability to get to 50 percent true instructional and interpersonal leadership behavior can be a real challenge.

For this reason, it is important for the leader to have grit and determination that for each and every new day, the goal remains the same. Even when yesterday, or perhaps even last week, resulted in a failure to get to 50 percent, the high-impact leader recognizes that just because a goal was not reached does not mean that the goal does not have value or cannot be reached today. Being goal driven is a prerequisite for high-performing leadership (Zenger and Folkman, 2002). One of those goals must be how to use time to achieve the primary mission of the organization.

TODAY IS A GOOD DAY TO GET TO 50 PERCENT

1. Today is a good day to review the calendar and add mission-driven activities to the agenda for the day. What gets monitored is more likely to get done. By looking at the day's activities in the context of management activity, technical activity, and mission activity, the leader can determine what percentage of his or her time is actually being spent on Tier 3 leadership activities.
2. Today is a good day to reprioritize work time around the mission, the "big yes." What is valued most should have the highest priority. Rebuild the schedule for the day, if needed, in order to prioritize time and effort toward the big mission, the big ideas.
3. Today is a good day to evaluate the calendar and see if the focus is on "problem space" or "solution space." It is easy for modern leaders to look more like firefighters than architects. By examining the degree to which the day is being spent reacting to issues rather than being proactive and strategic, the likelihood of moving more and more toward 50 percent of the day being spent on mission-building activities goes up.
4. Today is a good day to spend quality time with students. If the primary mission of the organization is to make a difference in the lives of children, it is important to be with those students on a regular basis. Too often, leaders are not communicating directly with students at all, or leader-to-student communication is limited to issues around safety and compliance.
5. Today is a good day to start a log of how leadership time is actually being spent. The leader's day is too hectic, too filled with multiple

meetings and events, for him or her to be able to accurately remember how much time has been spent on any given task or leadership tier. By keeping an accurate log of what activities actually occurred during the day, and how long those activities lasted, the leader can begin to build an accurate picture of how his or her time is spent.

6. Today is a good day to schedule nonnegotiable time out of the office and in the field. On any given day, the leader's calendar will include meetings that must be attended. The leader knows that the meeting with the boss or the faculty meeting is nonnegotiable. When leaders also build nonnegotiable time out of the office and in the field, where the students and teachers are, the likelihood of getting to 50 percent Tier 2 and Tier 3 activity increases.

Chapter Six

Brush Off the Chips

As we discussed in chapter 4, getting to Tier 3 leadership involves building expertise in the behaviors and attributes that define interpersonal skills and team-building activities. Tier 3 leaders recognize that high-impact leadership is fundamentally a "people enterprise." The ability to motivate, influence, understand, and leverage the personalities and motivations of a large group of diverse people around a common mission is the goal of every individual wishing to function as a Tier 3 leader.

There are specific behaviors that leaders who are recognized as highly skilled in the ability to motivate and influence others display on a regular basis. Scholars in the field of leadership development such as Zenger and Folkman, among many others, have spent a great deal of time studying the interpersonal skills and behaviors that leaders need to cultivate in order to influence others through team building, communication, and individual capacity building.

Interpersonal skills such as inspiring and motivating stakeholders, developing others, building relationships, and collaborating in meaningful ways with team members are all examples of key interpersonal skill competencies (Zenger & Folkman, 2002). There is also a strong relationship between the attitude that leaders have toward the work and stakeholders' attitudes toward the work. When leaders demonstrate a positive attitude toward change and toward establishing organizational goals in a collaborative fashion, stakeholders' commitment to promoting a positive learning environment for students also increases (Abdullah & Kassim, 2011).

In addition to building a repertoire of positive interpersonal skills and behaviors, Tier 3 leaders also need to develop the ability to avoid negative behaviors and attitudes toward individuals who are hostile to the leader's goals or actions. All leaders must deal with stakeholders who are not team players, who are actively opposed to the leader's point of view, who have competence issues, or who are simply behaving poorly. It is easy for leaders to develop negative attitudes toward these individuals, whether they are students, teachers, parents, or any other active stakeholder in the system.

It is also easy for these attitudes to subtly shape the leader's ability to work effectively with these individuals. When leaders collect these "chips" and carry them around, the ability to positively impact, motivate, collaborate, and communicate with these individuals is weakened or eliminated altogether (Colwell, 2015). These negative "chips" do not go unnoticed by the leader's colleagues. Even those individuals with whom the leader has no issues and is working well can typically see the change in the leader's attitude, body language, and interaction when working with a colleague whom the leader perceives as hostile to the leader's agenda or to the leader himself.

Brushing off the chips that are certain to accumulate over time must be a daily strategy for impactful leaders. Brushing off the chips is not something that a leader does once and then has solved the problem. Because employees and stakeholders can, on any given day, appear to be obstacles to the leader's mission and the harmonious work of the team, simply recognizing that these behaviors on the part of some constituents are occurring is not enough.

Nor is it enough for the leader to make having a positive attitude, even toward those who are behaving unreasonably, a goal for the year or even the next month. Brushing off the chips of negativity and starting fresh with all stakeholders must be a daily activity. Leaders will be subjected to a negative attitude on a daily basis from someone. The leader's proactive response to such activity must also be a daily occurrence.

Tier 3 leaders recognize that there is no such thing as unanimity of purpose or spirit from all stakeholders, no matter how skilled the leader or how noble the mission. Most leaders are able to recognize the poor behaviors of others. Recognizing poor behaviors in others, however, is, in and of itself, not enough. The impactful leader also recognizes how those hostile or unprofessional behaviors are negatively affecting other colleagues and stakeholders each and every day.

More importantly, and often harder to diagnose and recognize, is the leader's ability to recognize that those negative behaviors are affecting the leader directly. Too often leaders consider themselves immune from the negative attitudes or behavior patterns that they easily see in others. Leaders can see who is having a negative impact on the team and the mission, and they can also see who is being impacted by those negative colleagues, but they sometimes cannot see that they themselves are also being impacted and changed by those same individuals.

Changes in leadership attitude toward specific stakeholders will certainly occur when the leader is not overtly working to compensate for the natural instinct to treat those who are supportive differently from those who are not supportive. These subtle, and not so subtle, negative behaviors from the leader toward certain individuals or groups of people not only limit the ability of the leader to influence and motivate all colleagues and stakeholders, but they are also very noticeable to those hostile to the leader or the leader's agenda.

Think about how common it is for some team members to be perceived as members of the leaders "A Team." Consider how stakeholders in most organizations would answer the following questions about the leader's attitude toward everyone in the organization: Does the school leader treat everyone the same, with the same courtesy and respect, as the most valued member of the organization? Does the school leader recognize when they appear to be "playing favorites" or when they are displaying a negative attitude, tone, or body language toward some members of the organization? For most leaders, it is inevitable that the answer to either of these questions would be "no."

If the answer to either of these questions is "no," then the leader needs to reflect on how their attitude and interpersonal skills are being perceived by everyone in the organization. The issue is not whether or not these attitudes are occurring between a leader and the other members of the organization. They are occurring.

Conflict will always occur in any human enterprise, and humans will always react differently to those who are supportive from those who are hostile. The issue is whether or not the leader recognizes that these conflicts and resulting behaviors are happening, and whether or not the leader is willing to take action to minimize, or prevent, these behaviors from changing how the leader interacts with the organization.

Because a wide variety of human interactions, both good and bad, will certainly be a daily occurrence for any leader, brushing off the chips must then also be a daily leadership behavior. Just because the leader adopted a fresh new attitude on Monday does not mean that that attitude will still be there on Tuesday. Like any meaningful and difficult task, adopting a fresh, positive attitude toward those who are not responding in kind requires daily discipline. Attitude is like trust. What has been built up over time can quickly be lost in a just a moment or a day. Trust is earned each and every day. Interpersonal skills are on display each and every day. For both trust and interpersonal skill development, inconsistency kills.

THE DAILY ATTITUDE INVENTORY

In the classic sitcom *Seinfeld*, George Costanza, one of the main characters, describes a special family holiday celebrated by the Costanza family, called Festivus. Among the many quirky customs of Festivus is something called the "airing of grievances," in which family members share the many ways they have been let down or disappointed throughout the past year.

Like the Costanzas, leaders typically are aware of the grievances of others. Like the Costanzas, most leaders are also keeping track (consciously or unconsciously) of the slights, omissions, and hostile behaviors of others. Employees, students, parents, and other stakeholders are quick to point out their concerns to the leader regarding any number of issues, big and small. In the age of social media, these stakeholder concerns are often also shared instantly with the larger community.

The issue for today's leaders regarding grievances is not usually a lack of understanding or awareness of the grievances of others, but rather a lack of leadership awareness of how those grievances are affecting the daily behaviors and attitudes of the leader. Too often, leaders fail to be self-reflective about their own grievances, their own attitudes, and how those attitudes are being perceived by others.

For school leaders striving to reach their potential as interpersonal skill experts, the Festivus tradition of the "airing of grievances" needs to be replaced with a new tradition: the "understanding of how the grievances of others affect daily leadership behavior." This is done by taking a quick, honest, and daily inventory of leadership attitude toward stakeholders who are behaving poorly in some way.

BE HONEST ABOUT THOSE WHOM YOU ARE UPSET WITH

Perhaps the biggest mistake leaders can make when dealing with the chips they are carrying is to believe that, in fact, they are not carrying any chips at all. In order to be successful, leaders need confidence. This confidence, however, can often result in a kind of blindness to certain behaviors or a belief that the leader is immune from carrying around grudges or treating people differently based on their past interactions.

These behaviors occur either from a lack of introspection by the leader or a failure by the leader to recognize that leadership behavior is being affected by past interactions with stakeholders. High-performing leaders, on the other hand, are self-aware, organizationally aware, and able to manage their own feelings. They do not react out of impulse and they have a high degree of empathy (Goleman, Boyatzio, & McKee, 2002).

Of the two leadership errors discussed above, a failure to honestly reflect about where organizational conflict is occurring and how that conflict is affecting the leader's behaviors and attitudes is the most common. In this case, the leader honestly believes that he or she is immune from such petty behaviors as carrying around grudges, or treating people differently when they are disagreeable or are behaving poorly.

As a result of this failure to recognize that everyone is impacted by how they are treated and that everyone needs to learn and practice how to treat each person with dignity and respect, particularly when that individual is behaving in a less-than-optimal fashion, leaders who fail to brush off the chips, because they are under the mistaken impression that they don't have any chips to brush off, are certain to struggle over time as Tier 3 leaders.

In order to brush off the chips on a daily basis, the leader must ask and answer truthfully several important questions:

1. Who in the organization is behaving in ways that the leader finds counterproductive, hostile, or irritating in some way? Recognizing who is reacting in a passive-aggressive manner or is overtly hostile to leadership or leadership initiatives is a relatively straightforward undertaking. If the leader is engaged with internal and external stakeholders on a regular basis, and is paying attention to how these colleagues are reacting to leadership behavior, the identities of those who have not bought in to the direction the leader is taking the organization should be clear.

   Only those leaders who find themselves isolated from the organization they lead may be unaware of which constituents have not accepted or supported leadership activity. Those isolated leaders are at great risk of becoming either irrelevant or incompetent when it comes to Tier 3 leadership success.

2. Does the leader recognize how they are reacting when working with these hostile or difficult individuals? The answer to this question can be much more complex than the answer to the previous question. Too often, leaders feel confident that they understand exactly how others within the organization are reacting to each other, what team dynamics are at work within the organization, and exactly how they, as leaders, are reacting to these interpersonal dynamics.

   Unfortunately, it is often easier to see the verbal behavior, body language, and responses that others demonstrate when interacting with colleagues with whom they disagree than it is for the leader to recognize those same behaviors in themselves. Tier 3 leaders recognize that it is human nature to have negative reactions toward stakeholders who are not cooperative or who are impacting the organization's mission in negative ways. Tier 3 leaders spend time in honest self-reflection about their own behaviors toward these individuals.

3. What are the verbal or nonverbal cues that the leader, is communicating when working with individuals who are not supportive? It is human nature to want to spend more time with those who share a com-

mon mission, attitude, and viewpoint than it is to spend time with those who do not share the same organizational views.

As a result, leaders will often begin to limit the amount of time spent communicating with the silent in the organization or with those openly hostile to the leader's viewpoint. For these leaders, a telling cue that this isolation is happening is to look at the leader's calendar.

Which individuals are meeting with the leaders and leadership team on a regular basis? What classrooms, department meetings, or committee meetings are the leaders visiting on a regular basis? For that matter, who are the individuals who serve on those committees or who lead the departments? Do leaders delegate to their subordinates activities that require interaction with those in the organization who are not supportive, in effect spending time only with the "yes men" within the system?

4. Do leaders tend to share their irritation about the behavior of other individuals with other members of the leadership team or with other constituents? For many leaders who are struggling with the stressful and complex task of leading a school or school district, the answer to this question is "yes."

Teacher lounge talk about "that" student or "that" parent is an all-too-common, and unfortunate, by-product of most school environments. Leaders will often discuss with faculty and staff the need to maintain professionalism and student/family confidentiality at all times. In cases like this, the leader is correct to recognize that gossip and conversation that is demeaning or that belittles any student or stakeholder associated with the organization is a sign of a lack of civility and professionalism that should be avoided.

PRACTICE WHAT IS PREACHED

For many leaders, however, the tendency to demonstrate the same unprofessional behavior can occur between the leader and members of the leader's trusted inner circle. Just as the teacher feels the need to vent or blow off steam regarding a parent or student who is causing problems for the teacher, so, too, can leaders easily find themselves speaking poorly or showing frustration about colleagues who are causing problems for them.

The "teacher lounge talk" that is so easily recognized by the leader as inappropriate and counterproductive becomes "administrator or leadership team talk" that mimics those very same negative behaviors. While the leader may not recognize that behavior in themselves, those around the leader will certainly recognize it.

By failing to understand the need for consistency between what is expected of others and what is expected of oneself, and by appearing to demonstrate a corresponding lack of character, the leader is failing to demonstrate fundamental leadership characteristics (White, 2008). Knowing that negative leadership attitudes toward others is visible and recognized by colleagues is an important step in learning how to brush off the chips.

BE PROACTIVE

Is the leader purposeful about removing the chips? In order to eliminate this all-too-human tendency to treat people differently based on how those people are perceived, the leader needs to be purposeful about the need to change their own behavior. If the leader is not willing to ask the question, "What can I do today to remove or reduce the negative tendencies and attitudes I have toward these individuals?" then it is unlikely that the behavior itself will diminish.

By asking trusted colleagues to call out the leader when this behavior occurs, and by honestly self-reflecting about one's own behavior, the leader can move each day toward being a role model who not only talks a good game about dignity and respect, but actually models that behavior.

By asking these questions each day and honestly answering them, the leader is well on the way to developing one of the most difficult leadership interpersonal skill behaviors to maintain: treating each and every stakeholder with dignity and respect each and every day regardless of who that person is and what that person's attitude is toward the leader and the leader's agenda.

ASSUME COLLEAGUES VIEW THE LEADER AS HAVING FAVORITES

Just as common of a leadership error as believing that there are no individuals within the organization that the leader is hostile toward is the belief that there are no leadership favorites, no "leader's pets" who receive preferential treatment or special access. Just as it is human nature to carry chips on one's shoulders about individuals who are difficult to work with, it is also human nature to want to surround oneself with like-minded individuals who are supportive of the leader's goals and mission. In fact, that is what high-performing teams typically look like: groups of individuals who share a common mission and purpose and who treat each other with dignity and respect.

All leaders want to, and need to, work closely with these supportive individuals, these "dancers." Providing these dancers with special treatment, treatment that others within the organization do not get, however, is not necessary. Building teams, developing a common mission of great worth, and accomplishing complex tasks in order to reach the larger goals of the organization is what the leader is there to support in the first place.

In chapter 12, there will be a thorough discussion on the importance of leaders' identifying the early adopters, the believers, the mission-driven colleagues, and the benefits of working with those dancers on a daily basis. The leadership danger lies not in aligning with and empowering these common-mission stakeholders, but in doing so to the exclusion of other stakeholders who don't yet share the common mission or who are actively opposed to the mission as presented. Of course, leaders need to dance with the dancers, but they also need to lead, influence, and support the more silent members in the system.

The tendency to surround oneself with clones, with positive mission-driven colleagues, and to remove oneself from interactions with colleagues who are hostile to, or unprepared to serve the mission, is powerful. That tendency to only dance with the dancers is also a Tier 3 leadership trap. Tier 3 leaders take the time each day to look at whom they are interacting with each day. And Tier 3 leaders consciously decide to spend time seeking the perspective of those with whom they disagree.

REACH OUT TO THOSE WHO ARE NOT SUPPORTIVE

Looking at, and understanding, the daily schedule is an important part of effective Tier 3 leadership. Understanding how time is spent is key to getting to 50 percent Tier 2 and Tier 3 leadership behavior (see chapter 5). Understanding how, and with whom, time is spent is also critical in understanding how chips on the shoulder may be impacting the leader's daily interactions. If Tier 3 leadership is built primarily around empowering quality teams through strong interpersonal skill sets, then who those team members are becomes important.

Is the leader's day being spent exclusively working with only like-minded colleagues? Who makes up the teams that are making the leadership decisions for the organization? Are the teams limited only to those early adopters of the leader's vision? Is there any interaction occurring that is meaningful with members of the organization or stakeholders who are not early adopters, or who are known to be opposed to the leader's agenda and actions? These questions need to be asked and answered by the leader on a daily basis.

The passing of time is not a friend to the leader who is carrying chips. It is too easy for days to become weeks and for weeks to become months in which there is no meaningful interaction between the leader and those individuals within the organization who are opposed to the leader in some way. It is too easy for the makeup of committees or leadership teams to be filled only with leader allies. The more time passes and the more entrenched the organization becomes with leadership favorites and leadership outcasts, the more difficult it becomes to build bridges between all stakeholders.

What is difficult, but necessary, in order to avoid the passage of time cementing these relationships as either positive or hostile, is to build into the daily schedule multiple opportunities for leadership interaction with stakeholders who are not natural allies. Tier 3 leaders reach out to those with whom there are disagreements or personality clashes, and they do so on a regular and purposeful basis. Tier 3 leaders reach out, not just for the purpose of being seen as working with everyone, but also because of a genuine desire to understand the perspective of others.

Communication with everyone requires effort and commitment on the part of the leader. Effective communication is a two-way street that connects all employees. By building daily opportunities for that communication to occur with all stakeholders, leaders are more likely to reduce conflict and misunderstandings and less likely to carry those chips on the shoulder that only weaken the leader's ability to influence all members of the organization in a positive way.

In summary, in the complex and stressful world of P–12 education, there will always be people by whom the leader feels mistreated in some real way. It is easy for that perceived mistreatment to change the leader's attitude and behavior toward certain stakeholders. Often, those changes in behavior can be subtle and not easily felt or understood by the leader, but those subtle differences in how the leader treats and interacts with others are seen and noticed by the stakeholders themselves.

In order to function at maximum effectiveness, high-impact leaders recognize that these chips exist, and they work to brush off these chips each and every day. They think about who or what has irritated or frustrated them during the previous day, and they make a commitment to start each day fresh.

Leaders who carry their chips around from day to day, gathering new ones along the way, will soon be weighted down with negative attitudes toward too many stakeholders. These chips become obstacles to the leader's interpersonal skill set, perhaps the most important set of skills needed for extraordinary leadership (Zenger and Folkman, 2009).

TODAY IS A GOOD DAY TO BRUSH OFF THE CHIPS

1. Today is a good day to positively reinforce the work of a mission adversary. Praise and recognition under any set of circumstances is a powerful thing. When that praise is directed at someone who is not

seen as a supporter of the leader and that praise is seen as genuine and deserved, the power of praise only grows.

2. Today is a good day to make a "reach out to" list instead of a "to do" list. Rather than thinking about things that need to get done, think about people who need to be heard from and supported.
3. Today is a good day to laugh at yourself. A sense of humor, particularly when issues are difficult and when the overall organization is under stress, helps to bring a sense of perspective to the organization. Leaders who can find humor in the inevitable follies of the organization, particularly in the leader's own errors, are seen as more approachable and more relatable to all stakeholders than leaders who don't know how to smile or to laugh.
4. Today is a good day to think about the criticism you are receiving and determine what truths exist in that criticism. It is easy to evaluate and provide critical feedback to others. It is a more challenging task to accept critical feedback from others in a reflective and thoughtful way. High-impact leaders recognize that criticism, when looked at seriously, can help the leader grow and understand how the leader is being perceived by others.
5. Today is a good day to examine the day's agenda and ensure that all voices are being heard. It is a common leadership trap to only listen to a small group of individuals or to only listen to individuals who are likely to agree with the leader's current thinking. Reach out to a new group of individuals or to a new category of stakeholders today.
6. Today is a good day to ask trusted advisors whether or not you are treating all stakeholders with the same level of dignity and respect. Many leaders honestly believe that everyone in the organization is treated with the same level of dignity and respect. Ask trusted colleagues whether or not they have the same perception.

Chapter Seven

Reduce Position Power Behavior

Every position in an organization comes with some level of position power, which is the power that comes explicitly with the position itself, regardless of who fills that position at any given time. Typically, as the level of responsibility rises for any given position, the level of authority, of power, embedded in that position also rises.

For example, principals have more position power than assistant principals, superintendents have more position power than principals, and so on. While there are many types of power—the power of expertise, the power of persuasion, the power of personality and charisma, to name a few—the power that is explicit as outlined in every job description is typically what leaders and subordinates think of when discussing the power of the position.

Clearly, school leaders at any level of the organization, from assistant principals to district superintendents, hold positions with high levels of responsibility. Common practice would dictate that as the level of responsibility rises within a given job, so, too, does the power of the position rise in order to ensure that the leader has all of the authority needed to carry out those job responsibilities.

While the level of position power for public school leaders is less than the commensurate amount of position power held by leaders holding jobs of similar scope and responsibility in the private sector, with the myriad of regulations and oversight that school leaders face, there is still a great deal of position power allocated to school and district leaders.

The power to hire, evaluate, retain, promote, and dismiss employees lies largely within the power of the school leader, as described in collective bargaining agreements and/or state statutes. Additionally, the power to establish teaching assignments, room assignments, and budget allocations are just a few examples of the power of the P–12 leader based on the authority granted by the position itself.

Position power exists for many reasons and clearly has its place in how high-performing leaders carry out their missions (Pierce & Newstrom, 2003). For many, position power is seen as a way to manage the organization in an efficient manner. Most would agree that chaos would ensue, and no timely, meaningful activity would occur, if every decision, every action, required a committee review or an organizational consensus before proceeding.

Many leaders use the power of the position to delegate specific tasks and activities to others throughout the organization. By distributing responsibility and authority to followers throughout the organization, with each individual tasked by the leader to accomplish specific objectives and to have a clear understanding of what tasks and goals they are responsible for achieving, and having those followers use the power delegated to them by the leader to accomplish those tasks, the organization can run smoothly and efficiently.

The wielding of position power can also be seen as a useful way of dealing with issues that may be unpopular but that need decisive action (Shamir & Shamir, 2017). Instead of "paralysis by analysis," or inaction as a result of a lack of direction or consensus on how to proceed, leaders can use position power to "force" the organization out of inaction or away from action that is believed to be contrary to the organization's mission. For leaders relying on the power of the position, it is this power that allows the leader to do what needs to be done. This is what the position-power leader is there to do. This is why the leader is given position power in the first place: to make the tough decisions.

THE LIMITS OF POSITION POWER

As in many large and complex organizations, however, the value and effectiveness of position power in the education leadership sector, as a primary tool for accomplishing the organization's goals and objectives, is rapidly diminishing. Modern complex systems in the private and public sectors operate in what was earlier described as VUCA environments—that is, environments that are volatile, uncertain, complex, and ambiguous.

If P–12 schools and school districts are in fact operating in VUCA environments, then P–12 school leadership in the twenty-first century must be a team sport. No one leader, regardless of their talent or commitment level, can impact an organization as complex as a school or a school district by themselves (Spillane, 2005). In twenty-first-century school leadership, it is the power of the team, not the power of the position, that has the greatest ability to impact.

What Wageman (2008) calls the "great group" idea is more than an opportunity for leaders to collaborate and involve as many stakeholders as possible in the leadership processes of the organization; it is a necessity. Even if one single leader could change the culture, climate, and performance of a school alone, it would not be through the power of their position, but through the power of their expertise and mission voice toward the organization's goals.

Impactful leaders purposely reduce the use of position power. Impactful leaders don't lead through "royal decree," or a series of commands to their subordinates (Zand, 1997). Tier 3 leaders recognize that reducing the use of position power, and increasing the use of expert power and the power of influence and persuasion through the use of mission-driven interpersonal skill sets, must be a daily goal for every leader.

These leaders recognize that the authority that they seek in order to lead comes not from the power of the position, but from the ability to demonstrate to all stakeholders their worthiness as a servant-leader (Greenleaf, 2002). Just as the need to focus on "brushing off the chips" is an activity that must be prioritized and acted upon on each day, so, too, is the need to focus on reducing position power, which entails a series of events and behaviors that must occur and reoccur each day.

With the important exception of issues dealing with school safety and ethical or criminal activity, the use of position power to get things done is counterproductive. A fundamental Tier 3 leadership behavior then relies on leadership understanding and implementation of strategies and behaviors that reduce the use of position power and increase the use of expert power and the interpersonal skill power.

BUILD DIVERSE TEAMS AND TASK THEM WITH IMPORTANT WORK

Impactful leaders use the power of the position to distribute leadership to, and increase the capacity of, the team (Harris, 2004). In effect, Tier 3 leaders use the power of the position to reduce the amount and scope of that power being used by the leader, and they purposefully distribute that power to the team, in effect reducing the leader's own power. For this distribution of leadership to be impactful and meaningful, it must be much more than the delegation of tasks. Delegating tasks is often just the use of position power by the leader, not the distribution of position power to others.

Too often, those delegated tasks are menial in nature, and they have a daily operations and a Tier 1 management focus. Too often, the delegation also comes with so many strings attached regarding how to accomplish the task, with whom to accomplish the task, and when the task must be completed, that any opportunity for creativity or critical thinking—of true leadership, in other words—on the part of the individual or individuals delegated with the task, is lost. In cases like these, delegation becomes routine management work, or work that the leader would rather have someone else do.

This behavior is top-down in its decision-making orientation and predicated upon the ability of the leader to order the completion of the task based simply on the position of power held by the leader. Delegation of routine tasks without delegating authority or delegating more significant tasks, but then micromanaging those assigned to complete the assignments, is not an example of reduced position power; it is just another example of position power in action. In fact, any delegation of routine tasks, even when given the responsibility and authority to carry out those tasks, is still an example of the use of centralized position power.

Building and empowering teams with important and meaningful work does not involve the delegation of tasks, but the distribution of leadership decision-making. This type of distributed leadership requires trust by the leader. Chapter 9 focuses on the significance of trust in any high-performing organization, and the significance of that trust starting from the leader and moving down through the organization. More important still, the potential of the distributed work to make a meaningful difference to the culture and goals of the organization is an important prerequisite for diffusing the use of position power by the leader.

The meaningful distribution of leadership and the development of leadership teams require several crucial components: First, the authority to access all of the resources of the organization to accomplish the mission must be present for the team. Sharing power means sharing the resources that come with that power. Empowering others to tackle important and complex work without providing the time, financial resources, and access to information necessary for a reasonable opportunity to succeed is not team building. Just as every leader expects to be given as much support as possible from their superiors, so, too, will the leadership teams empowered with meaningful work expect, and need, the same level of access to resources.

Second, the mission itself must be meaningful and significant. Giving a team all the resources and authority necessary to accomplish routine school operations may be effective delegation, but it is not effective distributed leadership. A critical element of distributed leadership is embedded within this concept. No matter how much authority and responsibility is granted to others within the organization, if the delegated task itself is menial or managerial, then the outcomes will clearly be menial or managerial. Delegating Tier 1 activity may result in the distribution of Tier 1 responsibilities, but it does nothing to distribute Tier 2 and Tier 3 leadership responsibilities.

Teams don't just want to be there to carry out instructions; they want to be able to have some input, some involvement, in creating the plans (Tredgold, 2016). The ability for the team to work on areas of significance, of challenge, to the organization is what separates the leader who professes to share leadership responsibilities through delegation, from the leader who actually distributes leadership through teams empowered with meaning. Chapter 8 explores in detail the power of meaning, of work that is significant, as a primary resource for high-performing leaders, as well as a powerful motivator for the organization's stakeholders.

BUILD EXPERT POWER BY ASKING LOTS OF QUESTIONS

If effective and sustainable power in twenty-first-century school organizations does not reside exclusively in the authority of the position, where can effective leadership power come from? One important source of power, which does not require the authority granted by the position itself, comes from the expertise of the leader. There is a reason the saying "knowledge is power" is so often used by teachers when working with students. There is a reason there is such a strong correlation in our society between the level of education attained and the level of income and responsibility earned.

The ability to have technical or expert power regarding the organization being led is not only a more impactful type of power than position power, but it is also a prerequisite type of power for any Tier 2 and Tier 3 leadership activity. There is no such thing as a high-performing instructional leader who doesn't have expert power in the field of teaching and learning. There is no such thing as a high-performing interpersonal skill leader who does not possess expertise in the fields of communication, motivation, mission building, and team building.

The first step leaders must take in building this important set of Tier 2 leadership skills is to become inquisitive, to inquire on a daily basis. High-performing leaders believe in the power of inquiry not only to improve their own understanding of the work to be done but also as a tool that grows the capacity of the entire organization. In this capacity, the leader is working to develop a culture of inquiry, not just for the leader but for all stakeholders (Copland, 2003).

When a culture of inquiry is built, everyone in the organization benefits. Teachers who work with leaders who are committed to developing the professional growth of everyone in the organization are more likely to collaborate and become inquiry-based, lifelong learners themselves (Blasé & Blasé, 2000). Asking questions of all stakeholders, and being interested in the answers, is not only a great way to start the journey toward greater expert power and the reduction of position power; it is also the only way to stay current in the field. Lifelong leaders, leaders who make a difference that is sustained, are also always going to be lifelong learners.

Being an inquiry-based leader, a leader who wants to know more today than was known yesterday, is first and foremost based on a state of mind. It is a leadership mind-set, an attitude toward the work, toward the people involved in the work, and toward the purpose of the organization. What all experts have in common is a strong commitment to the value of inquiry.

Experts are not smarter or more innately intelligent than most people. They are, however, more interested and more focused on asking questions and finding answers than most people. It is not the leader's role to know all the answers on behalf of the organization and its stakeholders. What is fundamental to the job, however, is the ability to ask the right questions. Impactful leaders are interested leaders. That interest is manifested, in large part, by a daily commitment to inquiry.

READ, STUDY, LEARN

Position power may give the leader the microphone, but that does not mean the leader has something meaningful to say. Too often, teachers, students, or any stakeholder can be heard saying the following about a leader: "He/she doesn't know what they are talking about." Pretending, or simply winging it, in areas of professional inquiry and leadership is not productive; it is, in fact, counterproductive. The irony is that the leader who pretends to know something is actually in a much weaker position, in terms of building expert power and reducing position power, than the leader who readily admits that the answer is not known or fully understood.

There is a real power that comes from honestly acknowledging that holding a leadership position does not, in and of itself, mean leadership knowledge of all things. Colleagues and stakeholders are much more receptive to following and joining leaders who are transparent about what they know and what they don't know. The power of saying "I don't know" is maximized when the leader quickly follows up by saying, "Let's find out." It is the finding out that matters, and the best way to find out is to read, study, learn, and practice.

What are the behaviors that make anyone an expert? What does it take to become at first proficient, and then an expert, in any particular field of inquiry or at any particular set of skills? It takes practice, it takes observational skills, it takes desire and perseverance, but most importantly, it requires leaders to see themselves as, first and foremost, daily learners. "A man who does not read has no appreciable advantage over the man who cannot read" (*Acknowledgment to the Dodge Idea*, 1914).

VOLUNTEER

An excellent way to reduce position power and learn how to lead through the power of expertise and a commitment to the mission is to join organizations in which there is no position power. By volunteering for committee assignments that are outside the scope and responsibilities of the leader's current position, the leader must learn to rely on expert power, interpersonal skills, and the ability to become a valuable and functioning member of a new team.

Learning to follow and become an effective and valuable follower is just as important of a skill set as learning to lead and become an effective leader. Leaders with no followers are not leading anything at all. In fact, many would describe a leader with no followers as delusional.

High-performing followers also have leadership skills. Leadership and the ability to influence others is not constrained or limited solely to those with position power (Goleman, Boyatzis, & McKee, 2013). Followers with no leadership skills or mission focus, however, are not impactful in any meaningful way to the goals of the organization or team; they are just along for the ride.

Joining and following others in the larger organization who are committed to the same organizational goals is an excellent way to learn how to influence through the power of ideas rather than the power of the position. Joining and following other committed members of the larger organization is an excellent way to develop the skills needed to be a team member, not just a team leader. Practicing and developing the power of expertise and the power of interpersonal skill development outside of the framework in which the leader has position power can only help the leader when he or she is operating within the framework of the power of the position held.

LEAD FROM THE CIRCLE

Organizational charts typically look like vertical pyramids. At the top of the pyramid one particular position resides—the president, the CEO, the chairman. Communication paths between and among employees in these pyramidal structures are typically vertical, as well. At each rung of the pyramid, someone is reporting up or delegating down to other employees based solely on where that person resides in the organizational structure.

In these vertical bureaucratic structures, it is the power of the position that controls the ability to communicate and the direction that communication will take. In the pyramid, the power of the position controls the flow of communication, the tone of communication, and the content of communication. In pyramidal organizational structures, there will be many employees who literally never work directly with, or in some cases seldom even see, those leaders at the highest rungs on the ladder.

For purposes of management efficiency and the clarity of job roles, this type of twentieth-century structure can be very efficient. Tier 1 management activity can be facilitated and streamlined through this type of organizational structure. For the purposes of creating organizational flexibility, critical thinking, and complex problem solving in environments that are volatile, uncertain, complex, and ambiguous, however, these same strict lines of command, control, and communication are not only inefficient, but they limit the ability of the organization to accomplish its primary mission.

One could even say these types of organizational structures limit the ability for many employees and stakeholders to even understand the mission. How often employees are heard lamenting the decisions being made by the "big bosses," or questioning whether those same leaders have any understanding of what is going on in the trenches.

A solution to this type of restricted vertical communication pattern is to organize the team, not as a vertical pyramid, but as a flat circle. High-impact leaders committed to reducing position power lead not from vertical pyramids, but from flat circles. A team working and communicating toward a common mission from a circular orientation sees each and every member of the team as having an equally important and valuable voice. It is not position power that determines the strength of that voice or the importance of that voice, but rather the simple fact that each member of the team, the circle, is there because of his or her expertise and commitment to the mission.

In the circle, authority and power are distributed. In the circle, each voice has some degree of real power and influence, regardless of the individual's position in the organizational hierarchy. In the circle, it is the ability to persuade, to influence, to demonstrate expert power, that carries the most weight. Leaders who operate from a circular, flat organizational framework rather than a vertical pyramidal framework will find themselves using position power less, and expert power and interpersonal skill power more. In the circle, the smartest person in the room, is the room.

THE SAFETY/ETHICS EXCEPTION

Of course, position power exists within every organization, and for many reasons. Someone must be in charge and ultimately responsible. The teacher in the classroom, the principal in the school, the superintendent in the district, all have position authority. Regardless of the leader's commitment to flat organizational structures and to shared leadership, every organization must have leaders who have the power of the position and the authority to use that power. Despite having this position power, impactful leaders approach each day with the goal of limiting the need to use the power of their position to get things done.

For most leaders, this daily goal will not be met. Position power will be used for almost all areas outside of the aspects of safety or ethics. Like attempting to get to 50 percent Tier 2 and Tier 3 activity each day, it takes grit to recognize the value of working toward these goals on a daily basis even when the goals seem out of reach. Impactful leaders continue to work toward reducing the use of position power on a daily basis, even if on most days that goal is not realized, because impactful leaders recognize that expert power and interpersonal skills are much more effective leadership behaviors than behaviors based solely on the power of the position held.

There are two important exceptions, however, in which the leader's use of position power is not only appropriate, but should be considered mandatory. These exceptions for the use of position power to accomplish organization goals involve issues dealing with the safety of employees and all stakeholders—both physical safety and emotional safety—and involve issues dealing with violations of organizational ethics and violations of law.

When threats to the physical and psychological safety of any stakeholder become apparent, the proper response from the leader should be immediately to take action to reduce or eliminate those threats. The response to a crisis involving the safety of students, faculty, or other stakeholders is not to schedule a committee meeting, survey colleagues for their ideas and suggestions, or make a new "to do" list. Leadership teams can meet later to review the cause of these threats and discuss ways to respond more effectively in the future.

The use of expert power, the power of the team and interpersonal skills to build systems so that the safety of everyone in the organization is monitored and assessed, must occur and can only occur successfully through the power of the team. Long-range planning, monitoring of organizational climate and culture, building redundant systems to increase security, and creating systems to respond to threats to safety are all best addressed through the strategic planning of the team. Responding to a real-time event, however, requires immediate action from the leader.

Clear violations of the law or the organization's code of ethics is a second area in which the use of the power of the position should be used by the leader. A leader who witnesses ethical or criminal events must take action. It is an effective and appropriate use of position power to remove the individual from the situation if violations of the code of ethics are being witnessed or reported. Contact law enforcement to investigate if the issue involves potential child abuse or any other potential criminal offense.

As with issues involving the safety and security of the organization, there is a place for the team to study, understand, and plan for responding to ethical and criminal violations by employees and stakeholders. That deliberative work should occur both before and after an event occurs. During the event itself, however, the use of position power is an appropriate response. In short, high-performing leaders use position power to deal with issues of safety (both physical and emotional) and to deal with issues of ethics or violations of the law. For everything else, high-impact leaders use expert power and mission (interpersonal skill) power.

Reducing position power can be a difficult and ongoing challenge for any leader. The willingness and effort needed to reduce the use of position power must be addressed on a daily basis. Just as getting to 50 percent Tier 2 and Tier 3 behavior is a challenging, and often never fully realized goal, so, too, does the challenge of drastically reducing position power as the means for accomplishing objectives and influencing behavior require daily vigilance.

TODAY IS A GOOD DAY TO REDUCE POSITION POWER

1. Today is a good day to empower both colleagues and stakeholders with meaningful responsibilities and opportunities to make a difference. Delegation without authority and responsibility or delegation only of managerial tasks is not an effective way to reduce position power. When leaders trust the team, they delegate significance. When teams are given significant responsibility and the tools and expertise to accomplish those missions, positive organizational climate and culture grows.
2. Today is a good day to distribute leadership responsibilities to the team. In the volatile, uncertain, complex, and ambiguous (VUCA) world of education, it is only the power of a committed team that will make a lasting impact on the organization. When the team is active and involved, success increases.
3. Today is a good day to give someone else the microphone. The smartest person in the room, is the room. Let the room speak. Let others lead, and let others take the initiative and receive credit for a job well done.
4. Today is a good day to add new members to the leadership team. When the team gets bigger, when more voices are heard, the likelihood of success increases. While it may seem more cumbersome to lead large groups rather than small groups, the culture of and the climate of the organization are not built and maintained by a small group of isolated leaders, but by all of the stakeholders in the organization.
5. Today is a good day to be a listener. Effective leaders are effective communicators. These leaders recognize that communication is not

just talking, explaining, or influencing, but also listening and understanding the points of view of others.
6. Today is a good day to seek out meaningful and actionable feedback. Process monitoring and progress monitoring are critical to any system committed to continuous improvement. Quality feedback is the cornerstone of continuous improvement. High-impact leaders don't wait for the feedback to come to them; they seek it out.
7. Today is a good day to be an effective follower. Without followers, there are no leaders. Every follower is setting a leadership example for someone, and every leader should be following a mentor, an expert in the field.
8. Today is a good day to be influenced by a respected colleague. Never underestimate the power of influence as a leadership skill. Recognize that influence, however, is a two-way street. Be just as willing to be influenced as to be an influencer.
9. Today is a good day to learn something new and increase expert power. When leaders are not learning, they are no longer effective as leaders. Expert power is not a place or a destination; it is a journey.

Chapter Eight

Find and Use a Mission Voice

While most leadership job descriptions give the leader real power and authority designed to assist the leader in accomplishing the job, the research is clear that leaders who over-rely on the power of the position are unlikely to succeed. Position power usually comes with the authority to evaluate employee job performance, which directly impacts the ability of employees to retain their jobs, receive pay raises or promotions, and so forth. Position power also allows leaders to delegate tasks and to control the agendas for meetings or the work assignments and calendars for many employees.

Leadership positions also come with great responsibility. It is the leader, after all, who will be held accountable for the overall health of the organization and the ability of the organization to accomplish its goals and objectives. If the leader is going to be held accountable, then the position should provide the leader with the necessary authority to carry out the mission. While accountability and responsibility without authority would certainly add great stress to any job, the use of authority to accomplish mission objectives is limited at best and counterproductive at worst (Hatcher, 2010).

While the use of the power inherent in the position is not a successful long-term leadership strategy, it is also clear that there will be times when position-power activities will need to occur. It is inevitable that at some time every leader will face situations in which a quick decision must be made. Because decisions of this type—decisions that are urgent and time sensitive—require someone with position authority to respond, it is the leader who will typically be asked to make those decisions. When leaders use the authority given to them through the power of their position in an appropriate manner, the respect of followers can actually be strengthened (Shamir & Shamir, 2017).

Too often, however, leaders will make arbitrary decisions and announce those decisions based on a perceived emergency requiring the need for an urgent response, which, in fact, is not actually urgent at all. Decisions made in an authoritarian fashion about emergencies that are not really emergencies at all will quickly be seen by stakeholders as poor decision-making. These types of "emergency" leadership decisions are typically made alone and quickly.

Unfortunately, decisions made in isolation are almost never the best decisions, and they are often decisions that don't generate as much buy-in and cooperation from stakeholders. Decisions made quickly are also typically not the best decisions. Finally, decisions that seem urgent at the time are often, in fact, not that urgent and can be vetted by the larger leadership decision-making team. The trap that leaders must avoid is seeing every unexpected event as an emergency event and thus using the power of the position as the authorizing tool for decision-making and the mechanism used to achieve employee and stakeholder cooperation in meeting the leaders' goals.

SAFETY AND ETHICS

As discussed earlier, there are two fundamental areas of leadership responsibility in which the use of position power is most appropriate. First, position power is an effective tool for leaders when dealing with issues that involve the physical or psychological safety of students and employees. When specific events occur that clearly jeopardize student or faculty safety, or when the safety of any employee or stakeholder is at risk, leaders should not hesitate to use all of the authority vested in their positions to act immediately and decisively regarding the issue at hand.

Learning and teaching cannot occur in environments that are not physically and emotionally safe. The overall safety of all students and stakeholders is, in fact, job number one for every education leader.

Second, position power should be utilized by the leader when a clear and present violation of the profession's code of ethics, or legal violations of any type, are occurring. When the leader is aware of ethical or legal violations and is not immediately responding, the leader is guilty of a dereliction of duty. Leaders have the authority and the responsibility to use the power of the position to intervene; high-performing leaders use that power to protect the character and integrity of the organization itself.

The use of position power is not typically, however, the most effective leadership tool in the complex environment that is today's education system. What tools, what authority, what "voice" does the high-impact leader then need in order to lead effectively? What skills and attributes can the effective leader rely on to ensure that the objectives and goals of the organization are met?

These are fundamental question that every leader must be able to answer. If the leader cannot rely on position power as the reason that followers will follow, then what is the answer to the question, Why should anyone be led by you? If stakeholders and employees are not going to follow the leader based on the power of the position, then why are they going to follow the leader?

The answer to this question lies in the ability of the leader to use more than just a "position power voice"; he or she must also be able to use "expert power voice" and, most importantly, a "mission power voice." Leaders clearly have position power, and they will need to exercise that power from time to time.

Leaders also should be expected to have expert power, the ability to understand at a deep level what good teaching and learning looks like. After all, the educational leader is leading a teaching and learning system. The importance of expert power is discussed in depth in chapter 3. In addition to position power/voice and expert power/voice, however, the leader must have what this author calls "mission power/voice."

POSITION POWER VOICE

One of the interesting aspects of being a school or district leader, and having the requisite position power that comes with that leadership position—whether it is the position of first-year assistant principal or the position of the superintendent of schools—is that everyone knows and understands the power that comes with those job titles. Leaders do not need to announce that they have the power that comes with the position. Leaders do not need to "throw their weight around."

The power of the position, and the person who holds that position, is known by all of the stakeholders within the organization, both internally and externally. When the superintendent or the principal enters the room, those present understand that that individual is in a position of power. In fact, most stakeholders assume that school leaders have more authority, more position power, than actually exists within the job description, and most stakeholders are likely to be deferential toward the person in power.

The power of the position is certainly one of the advantages that leaders have. The less it is used, however, the more advantageous the leader's position actually becomes. As mentioned earlier, there is a time and a place for leadership use of position power. Those times, however, should be limited. When leaders encounter behavior within the organization that will lead to the physical or psychological harm of any employee or student, the leader should take charge and use the power of the positon to intervene. When a leader sees behavior that is clearly immoral or unethical, the leader should use the power of the position to intervene.

High-impact leaders, however, recognize that the modern age of school leadership requires the leader to build the capacity of the organization as a whole in order to be effective. Relationship-building, team-building, and mission-building activities, along with the effective use of expert power, are much more likely to result in organizational success than strategies based on a hierarchical leadership structure that is enforced by the power of the job itself.

EXPERT POWER VOICE

High-impact leaders understand the benefits and the limitations of position power. These leaders recognize that there is much more to being a high-performing leader than simply managing the organization or using the power of the position to delegate tasks or order compliance. These leaders recognize that improving learning outcomes for students requires a level of expertise that does not automatically come with the position (Leithwood, Begley, & Cousins, 2005).

Every complex organization is built upon a set of unique skills, unique vocabulary, unique goals, and unique best practices. Whether the leader is in charge of a large hospital, an airport, a construction company, or a comprehensive high school, there is a specific and unique set of skills and knowledge needed to be considered an expert in that field.

Expert power brings instant credibility to the leader's voice. When followers and stakeholders are confident that the leader "knows what they are talking about," success is much more likely to occur. When a leader is truly considered to be an expert in their chosen profession, there is a great deal of confidence and trust that stakeholders and colleagues will attach to the leader's point of view, simply as a result of the leader's perceived expert power on the subject at hand.

Likewise, leaders who are not experts, who are not lifelong learners, will quickly be perceived by everyone within and outside of the organization as lacking credibility. No one is interested in following leaders they believe do not know what they are talking about.

In the education sector, the primary mission of the organization is clearly centered on teaching and learning. Understanding what good teaching looks like, understanding how children learn, knowing how to assess the quality of instruction and learning that is occurring in a school or a school district, are all necessary skill sets for the modern P–12 education leader.

A leader cannot lead an organization when the leader does not understand the academic vocabulary upon which that organization operates. A leader cannot lead an organization without having a deep understanding of what are considered the best practices for that particular sector. A leader cannot lead an organization without understanding what the definition of "success" is and what success looks like.

When the leader does understand, in this case, what great teaching and learning looks like and is able to articulate that understanding in clear and consistent ways, the leader is relying on expert voice, on expert power, to move the organization forward. For the leader who relies on expert power to lead, the answer to the question, "Why should anyone be led by you?" is, "Because I am an expert in the field."

Expert power is not something bestowed upon a leader the way that position power is given to the leader, as a by-product of the job itself. Expert power, by its very nature, is earned. There is a reason there are so few "experts" in the world on any topic or in any sector. The time, the commitment, and the passion needed to build a deep understanding of any complex topic can be daunting. Few choose to do what it takes to get to expert power. High-performing leaders, however, take the time and make the commitment to become experts in their field.

Expert power is also dynamic. That is, someone with expert power ten years before may no longer be an expert in that same field ten years later. Expert power requires leaders to constantly change and update their own learning and understanding of the profession. Best practice changes, technology changes, and conceptual and practical understandings of what works and what doesn't work all change over time. Particularly in the field of education and pedagogy, when the leader stops learning, it is only a matter of time before the leader loses expertise in the field and then quickly loses credibility with the organization's stakeholders.

High-impact leaders make it a top priority to be lifelong learners. These leaders are constantly reading and participating in professional development in order to stay on the leading edge of innovation and understanding what best practice is in today's school environments. As discussed in chapter 11, Tier 3 leaders focus on process. One of the processes on which these leaders remain focused is how to ensure ongoing systems and behaviors that result in continuous learning and a current state of expertise.

Perhaps the single greatest attribute of leaders who maximize the power of "expert voice" in their daily leadership work is a daily commitment to inquiry. In this sense, being an expert is not the *ability* to know more about a particular subject than anyone else; rather, it is the *drive* to want to know more about the subject than everyone else. Experts don't *answer* more questions than everyone else; they *ask* more questions than anyone else. The ability to embrace a sense of inquiry will be discussed further in chapter 14.

Chapter 8
MISSION POWER VOICE

While position power has its place and expert power is a fundamental prerequisite for leadership success, it is the power of belief in a meaningful and impactful mission that truly motivates people. It is this third tier of leadership skill, the ability to lead via a mission-driven leadership voice, that matters most. While position power may result in employee compliance and expert power may produce better employee understanding of an issue and the belief that the leader knows what they are talking about, there is something very powerful and rewarding for employees and stakeholders alike when there is a strong belief that something of importance, of significance, has occurred because of one's efforts.

Leaders who can articulate, demonstrate, and lead teams of colleagues and external stakeholders toward a common, powerful mission are leaders who recognize the impact of a meaningful mission, a shared vision, on the overall organization (Senge, 2014). In VUCA environments, the leaders who have the ability to motivate and influence teams toward accomplishing powerful objectives are the leaders who succeed.

Leaders who hold and demonstrate deeply held beliefs and commitments to the primary mission of the organization are seen as charismatic figures who are committed to a worthy and meaningful set of goals. These leaders don't need to be extroverts to be seen as charismatic. Mission-driven leaders do, however, need to be able to demonstrate a mission voice, a mission-driven orientation toward the work.

Leaders who use a mission-driven voice need to be seen consistently by all stakeholders as caring deeply about the primary mission of the organization they lead. These leaders may be great public speakers or they may be quiet and introspective, but they all have one leadership attribute in common: All mission-driven leaders are committed to team oriented solutions and believe deeply in the importance of the work itself.

All stakeholders are much more likely to accept the leadership of someone who clearly believes in, and is able to articulate, the greater mission, the purpose of the organization, than leaders who expect stakeholders to follow them simply because they are in charge (position power) or because they appear to know what is best in any particular situation (expert power).

There is an important distinction, however, between having a task orientation and having a meaningful mission voice. It is important, when looking at the leader's mission voice and mission-driven activities, to see whether or not the mission that the leader espouses provides real meaning to everyone connected to the organization. There is an important difference between routine organizational tasks and meaningful organizational missions. In the context of high-impact leadership and the use of mission voice, it is the power of the mission itself that matters.

All organizations have a multitude of tasks, of to-do lists, to accomplish. It is the leader's responsibility to ensure that those tasks are accomplished successfully. A review of any leadership job description will be filled with fundamental activities or task objectives. School leaders need to be able to ensure that the master schedule is in place and functioning smoothly. Leaders need to be able to successfully accomplish routine activities, such as having organized systems in place for student transportation, housing, and lunch schedules. Leaders need to ensure that all budgets are handled in an appropriate and timely manner. All of these tasks are important. All of these tasks need to be accomplished effectively and efficiently.

None of these Tier 1 management activities, however, brings profound meaning to the organization's stakeholders. While there can certainly be a sense of satisfaction, of accomplishment, in knowing that these Tier 1 tasks have been successfully accomplished, the routine nature of these types of activities, while they may be part of the "job," are not part of the "calling" of the organization.

Simply put, these activities do not, in and of themselves, make a difference in the lives of children. Individuals do not go into education because they want to be part of the best lunchroom management system or the best master testing schedule; they go into education because they want to make a difference in the lives of children.

Perhaps it is more accurate to say that, when thinking about the leader's use of mission power or mission voice, the power of a leader's mission voice is directly related to the power and meaning of the mission itself. In this case, "mission voice" is only an effective leadership tool if it is "meaningful mission voice."

Organizational missions that have real meaning are, in and of themselves, charismatic. The leader who is introverted will still be seen as a charismatic leader when the leader's mission is charismatic. That is, missions with meaning impact employees and stakeholders in an emotional way that does not occur when accomplishing important tasks but tasks that, in and of themselves, are routine. What charismatic, mission-driven leaders have in common is a message that resonates.

The charismatic leader is able to articulate a powerful message in a way that allows followers to believe in a future that is in some profound way better than the present. The research on teacher job satisfaction consistently finds that making a difference in the classroom for children, having students succeed academically and socially, is the primary motivator of teacher job satisfaction (Brunetti, 2001; Griffith, 2004).

While issues surrounding salary and working conditions can certainly impact teacher morale and job satisfaction in a negative way, it is teacher impact on students that motivates teachers in a positive way. The success of students—success that really transforms the lives of students, success that provides students with opportunities to choose and achieve meaningful futures—is what motivates all educators, from first-year teachers to veteran principals and superintendents (Colwell, 2015).

The charismatic, meaningful mission that will resonate with all stakeholders is the mission to make a difference in the lives of children. When the leader, through both word and action, is able to focus, to motivate, and to articulate this primary purpose and the real value and power that lies within that purpose, then and only then is the leader using mission voice.

For too many leaders, the ability to articulate a powerful reason for the organization's existence either does not exist or is not articulated. For many leaders, the ability to prioritize the calendar and the daily schedule so that significant leadership activities are under way, with the purpose of spreading the powerful and impactful mission that is at the core of the organization, does not occur. For today's education leader, even when position power is properly used and expert power is in place, the ability to demonstrate a powerful and sustainable mission voice is a prerequisite for employee motivation, job satisfaction, and performance (Wright, 2007).

MISSION VOICE STRATEGIES

Mission-driven leaders recognize and define what is most important about the work of the organization. This is part of the 50 percent rule, the daily commitment to prioritize Tier 2 and Tier 3 activity as at least as important as Tier 1 leadership activity, discussed in detail in chapter 5. Tier 3 leaders realize that a great deal of work is necessary to accomplish for the organization to run smoothly; however, that work, in and of itself, does not give the employees within the organization a profound sense of meaning.

By defining, recognizing, and most importantly, prioritizing those aspects of the work that make a difference in the lives of the students being served, and the colleagues and stakeholders who have joined the organization to make that real difference, the mission-driven leader can begin to separate out management activities being undertaken by the organization as necessary tasks but not the tasks that matter most.

By clearly articulating those activities that are prerequisite tasks designed to accomplish the mission but that are not, in and of themselves, the mission of the organization, the leader can begin to identify and articulate those activities that provide meaningful mission outcomes. In short, leaders cannot prioritize behaviors and events that focus on the primary mission of the organization if they don't understand what the primary mission of the organization is.

Once leaders have a clear understanding of those aspects of the work that constitutes meaning and significance to the organization, the leader can begin to explain and model that meaningful mission in terms that can be understood by various stakeholder groups. Having a clear understanding of what the primary mission(s) of the organization are is a fundamental prerequisite for mission-driven leaders.

A second, but equally important component for any leader with a mission-driven orientation toward the work is the ability to explain the mission in ways that make real sense to a wide variety of constituents, both inside and outside the organization. Clearly, if the leader has a meaningful mission and behaves, in word and deed, in ways that support that mission, but many stakeholders do not understand the mission, or what the leader means when the mission is discussed, the likelihood of that mission becoming embedded in the organization's culture is highly unlikely.

Missions are only powerful to the extent that they are understood. If the mission can be explained simply, then it can be understood. If it can be understood, it can be done. If it can be done, then it can be done successfully. That success begins with the leader's ability to explain clearly (Tredgold, 2017).

The need for the mission to be understood requires the leader to remain consistent to the mission objectives, parameters, and operating principles, while at the same time being able to communicate with all stakeholder groups. How a leader communicates to the PTA, or to the school board, or to the faculty about the mission to build a comprehensive school culture and climate around the principles of restorative practice, for example, will require the leader to have a situational understanding of each group's level of understanding and interest in the topic.

What the school board needs to know about the reasons school culture and climate are driving forces in the overall ability of the school to teach all children may be different from what the PTA or the faculty needs to know about the same topic. What the school board wants to know, and needs to know, for example, about using restorative practices as the guiding foundation to accomplish that culture/climate mission of the organization will also vary from what the business community wants to know about the same topic. For all of these stakeholder groups, however, the leader's mission remains constant. The leader's communication plan must be designed to maximize the likelihood that each group will understand the mission.

Leaders who use a mission voice share their belief in, and support of, the primary mission of the organization with everyone, each day. Relentless communication on issues that matter is a key component of Tier 3 interpersonal leadership behavior. Too many leaders spend the majority of their day communicating about Tier 1 management activity. Too many leaders fail to have a communication plan, or even to see the need to communicate, in both word and deed, as a primary leadership obligation and opportunity.

When communication is occurring with Tier 1 leaders, it is often connected to management activity, administrivia, or other tasks that are simply being delegated to or reported on. In this environment, meetings, large and small, become consumed with delegating management tasks, reporting on the progress of management tasks, evaluating the effectiveness of management activity, and on and on. If 70 percent, 80 percent, or even 90 percent of the leader's day, and more importantly the follower's day, is consumed with management activity, the leader's voice, by definition, is the voice of a manager.

Chapter 5 discusses this leadership trap and the need to "get to 50 percent" Tier 2 and Tier 3 leadership behavior. A critical part of that 50 percent is the time leaders spend advocating, clarifying, and building capacity within the organization toward the primary mission of the organization. All of these skills require interpersonal expertise. All of these skills require a commitment on behalf of the leader and the entire leadership team to prioritize powerful and prolific communication as a fundamental leadership activity.

There should be no doubt that in organizations in which the leader cannot articulate, and does not believe in, the power of the organization to change the lives of its students in profound ways, the likelihood that the organization will achieve that goal is highly unlikely. The leader has to believe it in order for the organization to achieve it. The leader has to live it in order for the organization to commit to it. The leader has to communicate it in order for the organization to understand it.

High-performing leaders align themselves with others who share the mission. If effective management activity and expert activity requires a team of managers and experts in our modern school environments, then mission-driven leadership must also be a team sport comprised of individuals who share in the belief of the organization to accomplish profound goals.

It is one thing for leaders to have, and use, a mission voice that focuses the organization on the goals and objectives that truly matter. That leadership voice can be powerful and charismatic. That leadership voice is often a prerequisite for organizational action. If leaders don't believe the mission, or can't explain the mission, then why would anyone expect other stakeholders in the organization to know and commit to the mission? It is another thing, however, for the leader to build the capacity throughout the organization for the entire leadership team to be able to share and demonstrate the same understanding and belief.

Even the most effective leader needs like-minded colleagues throughout the organization who both share the leader's commitment to meaningful mission activity and are able to communicate that mission. Chapters 12 and 13 discuss the strategies and attributes that leaders use to build teams of highly committed and empowered stakeholders.

Mission-driven leaders build systems that ensure that the organization is spending significant amounts of time on their primary mission. Many leaders operate in organizations that are bogged down in Tier 1 activity, but are not sufficient to accomplish the mission (which requires Tier 2 and Tier 3 activity). These are the organizations that can't get to 50 percent, or that may not even realize that they need to get to 50 percent.

When it comes to moving the school or district culture to one that is focused on Tier 2 and Tier 3 behavior, one thing is certain: Systems must be built that support employee and stakeholder involvement in Tier 2 and Tier 3 activities, systems that provide the time, and all of the necessary bureaucratic support structures, that provide the authority for leaders and followers to engage in meaningful work. Schools and districts that do not provide these structures and systems will remain bogged down in Tier 1 management activity.

Mission-driven leaders also build systems that help expand the belief in, and understanding of, the mission beyond the early adopters, the dancers, to the silent stakeholders in the organization. It is a priority for these leaders to make sure everyone in the organization understands the true purpose of the work and to provide all stakeholders with the opportunity to work toward it.

Most schools and school districts understand the value of building systems, establishing protocols, and developing rules and procedures for routine activities. What is missing is the commitment to building equally powerful systems to ensure that all stakeholders are at least as engaged in meaningful activities as they are in routine activities.

Where this does not occur, employees may be successfully completing tasks and checking off to-do lists, but they will not see themselves as engaged in a powerful mission. They will not see themselves as proactive, they will not see themselves as leaders, and they will not see themselves as making a difference.

Tier 3 leadership—that is, leadership that is focused on culture, climate, team building, and interpersonal skill development—is the leadership focus needed in today's modern education environment. Leadership that understands and uses mission voice and mission behavior must be a fundamental daily activity. It is, in the end, the power of the mission, not the power of the position, that matters.

TODAY IS A GOOD DAY TO USE MISSION VOICE

1. Today is a good day to take a moment and thank a stakeholder who is making a difference in the school. Tier 3 leaders recognize that not one single day should pass without some specific recognition from the leader to a stakeholder who is making a difference. This recognition

can be accomplished in a matter of moments, but the benefits will last for months and years.

2. Today is a great day to begin with a team mission-building activity. The team is the most important resource the leader has. Any time spent supporting the team is time well spent. Why support the team? Because without a team, there is no successful mission.
3. Today is a good day to update stakeholders on the purpose of the mission. When organizations are only focused on short-term objectives or on management activities, it is easy to lose sight of the big mission. Impactful leaders never let too much time go by without reorienting the team to the larger objectives of the school or the school district.
4. Today is a good day to assess the climate of the school. Tier 3 leaders are not afraid to question all stakeholders about the overall climate of the organization. These leaders recognize that, while they may hear concerns that they would rather not hear, it is important to understand everyone's perception of the current state of the system in order to understand what changes may need to occur.
5. Today is a good day to initiate a culture-building activity. Purposeful cultures can be built; they can be supported and guided. Culture will happen; the question becomes whether it will happen with the leader or without the leader.
6. Today is a good day to share a core value of your school culture with an external stakeholder group. The number of stakeholders who are external to the organization, who are not employees or students, is large and important.
7. Today is the perfect day to make a difference in the life of a child. This is the primary mission of any educational organization. This is the mission that matters. If the focus of the day is not on this mission, in very real ways, the potential of the day is lost.
8. Today is a good day to share your organizational pride with the community. If the leadership team is not proud of the work that is occurring in the building, why would those individuals outside of the building feel pride in the work that is occurring? Accomplishments matter. Sharing those accomplishments is an important part of sharing the importance of the work itself.
9. Today is a great day to inspire students. The potential of the students served in our nation's schools is limitless. Leaders who are focused on making a difference in the lives of the students they serve are also committed to challenging, motivating, influencing, and inspiring those students to be all that they can be.
10. Today is a great day to thank support staff throughout the organization who are working behind the scenes to make it all happen. It is

often the many support staff working quietly but tirelessly behind the scenes that make the infrastructure and systems of the organization work. These employees are often underpaid and underappreciated. While the leader may not be able to solve the first issue, the ability to solve the latter can be resolved.

11. Today is a good day to plan a celebration. It has been said that to understand an organization's culture, just look at what it is that the organization celebrates. Celebrating successes, large and small, helps build an organization's sense of purpose and accomplishment. Too often leaders are focused on what is not working, to the detriment of what is working.

12. Today is a good day to identify ten mission-driven colleagues in the organization. Colleagues who are highly committed to the mission of the organization are difference-makers. These colleagues can influence, support, and impact a wide number of colleagues and external stakeholders.

13. Today is a good day to make a list of everyone in the organization who shares the organization's mission. There are more dancers, or stakeholders, who support the organization, or who are ready to support the organization, than typically are involved directly with the leader on a daily basis. Leaders who take the time to identify these dancers are more likely to succeed.

Chapter Nine

Trust Down the Organization

Traditional organizational and decision-making structures operate like pyramids. The CEO, the president, and the superintendent all work and lead from the top of the pyramid. For most organizations, policy decisions, organizational goals, and strategic planning begin at the top and then work their way back down the system to employees who work in the middle or lower tiers of the pyramid. From there, mid-level managers oversee and delegate leadership directives to those at the lowest level of the organization.

It should be noted that, for most organizations, procedures are also in place to allow for feedback and suggestions from mid-level and entry-level employees to move back up the pyramid. This feedback may be informal, or it may include formal opportunities through surveys or meetings in which subordinates provide feedback to leadership about how things are going lower on the pyramid. The reports and information that come back up the organizational decision-making structure are often limited, however, to status reports regarding how leadership initiatives are going, as well as any reports of operational or personnel difficulties.

In pyramidal, tightly structured organizational frameworks, meaningful collaboration between those at the highest levels of the organization and those who work at the lower levels of the organization is rare. This type of structure is purposefully designed so that those at the top of the pyramid, the decision-makers, can adjust strategies, timelines, resources, and so forth, and send revised plans and directions back down the system in ways that ensure that command and control is maintained. As with any original business plans that are designed at the top of the pyramid, any revised leadership plans all have the same formal orientation for decision-making and communication. That orientation is a top-down orientation.

TRUST IN THE PYRAMID

The same top-down orientation also dictates how trust and relationships are built and maintained. The formal structure for the orientation of trust building, if strategically thought about at all by the leadership team, is built upon an expectation that the employees at the lower rungs of the organizational structure will "trust up" to the leaders who reside at the top of the pyramid, where all of the position power lives.

The leaders ask for, and expect, the trust of their subordinates, their followers. Some leaders will recognize the value of trust and ask their employees to trust that they have the organization and the employee's best interests at heart. Employees will hear comments from these leaders such as, "I am your new principal, your new superintendent; I need you to trust me. I promise I will not violate that trust."

In this scenario, the leader begins the professional relationship by asking to be trusted. Typically the leader who truly cares about the relationship will promise not to abuse that trust. Other leaders will simply assume that trust from below comes with the job, the power of the position. These leaders will not communicate directly at all with colleagues and subordinates about the nature of trust or the importance of trust as a critical component for effective teamwork.

In this view, the leader assumes that the leader's job description itself justifies trustworthiness. In this scenario, there are no discussions between leaders and followers about the nature or importance of trust as a component of organizational health or mission success; it is simply assumed that employees will place their trust in the goodwill and expertise of their leaders.

Yet the research is clear that there is a powerful relationship between the overall effectiveness of an organization and the degree to which trust, and the collaboration that results from trust, is a meaningful part of the organization's culture, climate, and leadership (Harris, 2003; Scribner, Sawyer & Watson, 2007). For any organization to undertake meaningful reform or accomplish difficult and challenging goals, there must be a high degree of motivation and a significant commitment to the mission that promotes the hard work and trust that is necessary (Leithwood & Jantzi, 2000).

Additionally, the more that systems operate with distributed leadership models, the more members of the organization are empowered to lead and the more distributed the nature of trust becomes (Wahlstrom & Louis, 2008). In other words, as leadership is shared throughout high-performing organizations, so, too, is trust shared throughout these systems. When only the principal, or the leader with position power, is making decisions, the ability to trust in that sole leader becomes magnified, for better or for worse.

When a large number of stakeholders are operating as leaders, the impact of trust, or a lack thereof, from any one individual is minimized. Many leaders do recognize, or learn over time, that trust must be earned. These leaders are committed to acting in a way that justifies the trust that has been granted to them by the organization's stakeholders.

Despite that commitment to earning trust, many leaders still begin the relationship between leader and follower by formally asking to be trusted as a matter of organizational structure and efficiency. These leaders recognize that they have been placed in positions of power, of responsibility, for a reason. They know that they have been empowered, have been trusted by their superiors, to facilitate the organization's mission. In order to do so, the leader recognizes the need to be trusted by the other members of the organization. The system then operates with the assumption that those at the bottom of the organization in terms of power and responsibility should begin each day by trusting those who lead them.

This is "trusting up" the organization, and it is the default direction for how trust begins for most leaders. Asking followers to trust those in power, however, is not the most effective way to build trust throughout the organization. Tier 3 leaders do not assume that trust is inherent with the power of the position. Tier 3 leaders do not assume that trust begins with the follower trusting the leader, but rather that it begins with an organizational structure that has the *leader* trusting the *follower*.

TRUSTING DOWN

While asking for and expecting trust to move up the organization is how most leader-follower relationships begin, truly great leaders don't begin by asking the people they work with to trust them. Another orientation for trust is available to every leader, and this orientation can start today. This orientation requires a shift in how leaders begin and maintain relationships through both words and action. In this orientation, the leader begins by trusting others, by "trusting down" the organization. Impact leaders begin each relationship, each day, by trusting others.

These leaders recognize that asking others to trust the leader places the obligation of communication, and of trust, on the subordinate, even when that trust has not yet been earned by the leader. Tier 3 leadership behavior does not begin by saying, "You can trust me." Tier 3 leaders begin their relationships by saying, "I trust you."

By telling and, more importantly, by showing stakeholders throughout the organization that they are trusted—trusted to do their best work each and every day, trusted to be committed to the team and to the mission, trusted to follow the rules and expectations of the organization—the leader sends an important message throughout the system. The leader who is trusting down is showing confidence in colleagues' ability to do their job well.

What motivates followers to act on behalf of the leader and the organization as a whole, and how the follower perceives the relationship with the leader, plays a fundamental role in the ability of the leader to be successful (Haslam, Reicher, & Platlow, 2010). The trusting-down leader doesn't expect that trust to be automatically returned by subordinates or stakeholders, but instead earned by the leader over time.

Trust is a powerful thing. Trust is a prerequisite for all other Tier 3 leadership behaviors. Cultures built on trust are much more likely to be mission driven and achieve their organizational goals (Dirks, 2000; Lee, Gillespie, & Wearing, 2010).

THE TRUSTING LEADER

The trusting leader is not working from the perspective of the organizational structure as a pyramid, but from the view that the organizational structure is a circle in which leadership is distributed and shared collectively by an empowered team (Pearce, Hoch, Jeppeesen, & Wegge, 2011). In this framework, position power is not highly valued and is rarely used by the leader. In this type of flat organizational structure, decision-making authority is widely distributed. In this structure, it is the power of the team that is valued more than the power of the leader or of any one team member.

Distributed leadership involves many people and is thus inherently more complex than non-distributed leadership. In order for any large team of leadership equals to succeed, all of the members of the team must be trusted. Too often, leaders who ask first to be trusted, and expect that trust from their subordinates, fear the consequences of beginning each day by trusting others rather than by being trusted.

These leaders ask themselves questions such as: How can a leader, who is responsible for the mission of the organization, delegate real autonomy and authority to members of the organization who have not yet earned the trust of the leader? How can the leader trust team members with whom the leader doesn't work or communicate regularly? How can a leader trust from a position of physical or intellectual isolation from the rest of the team?

The answer to all of these questions, of course, is that the leader cannot "trust down" the organization while operating from this perspective. These are the questions being asked, not from the leader who is a member of an organizational circle, but from a leader who is a member of an organizational pyramid.

When leaders begin professional relationships by trusting those with less position power, they are demonstrating not only a level of respect for, and confidence in, the employees who work for them, but they are also demonstrating a commitment to distributed authority and responsibility to the team.

This trust and respect will be returned by those with less position power back to the leader (Conger, Kanungo & Menon, 2000).

While it may be easy for leaders to have an intellectual understanding of the critical importance of trust in any healthy organization, and while the leader may understand that trust must be a two-way street, there are several critical daily behaviors that Tier 3 leaders, leaders who trust down the organization, utilize.

LEAVE THE PYRAMID AND JOIN THE CIRCLE: COLLABORATE

It has been said that a leader with no followers is seen by the world not as a leader, but as a lunatic. It is the followers, the early adopters, the believers in the mission and vision of the leader, that make a leader successful and impactful. Whether leading in an organization with a strict hierarchical structure and tight chains of command or a loose organizational structure with a widely distributed leadership model, without followers, leaders don't exist.

Impactful leadership in twenty-first-century schools, leadership that succeeds in making a difference in the lives of students, must be built upon the development of a common mission valued by all employees and nurtured through the power of interpersonal relationships. Those interpersonal relationships can only occur if the leader sees him/herself as one member of a trusted circle of leaders. In this circular orientation, position power is not important; it is expert power and a distributed commitment to mission that is most valued. The primary objective and skill set of the leader is the ability to influence colleagues and stakeholders (Pink, 2014).

Powerful leadership teams don't happen by accident. Trust does not happen by accident. Building, supporting, trusting, and empowering teams of individuals from throughout the organization all working together on a common mission requires a relentless leadership commitment to, and understanding of, the value of collaboration and trust as critical to organizational success. Countries around the world who are succeeding in advancing teaching and learning in the classroom recognize that collaboration between teachers is the single most effective way to increase student achievement and success in the classroom (Weil, 2017).

Leaders who are committed to mission-driven outcomes that are large in scope and significant in impact also recognize that collaboration is a prerequisite for leadership success. Collaboration builds trust. Collaboration increases expert power. Collaboration increases efficiency. Collaboration increases the likelihood of meeting organizational goals and benchmarks.

If this is the case, however, then why do so many systems remain committed to the pyramid with its tightly controlled and limited distribution of power and autonomy? Why do so many systems operate with leaders working and making decisions in isolation? Why do so many leaders fear leaving the pyramid and joining the circle? While there are many answers to these questions, how the leader views the primary leadership role—as a Tier 1, Tier 2, or Tier 3 leader—has a lot to do with how the leader organizes the school or school district.

BEGIN BY TRUSTING OTHERS: TRUSTING THE TEAM

As discussed earlier, once a team-oriented structure has been established, leaders functioning in the circle must empower colleagues with true decision-making authority and responsibility. This requires trust from the leader to the team. For trust to remain between leaders and between leaders and followers, that trust must be validated consistently and over time. Trust maintained over time requires all parties to invest in the relationship and the work of the organization in an honest, transparent manner.

Certainly every leader will encounter individuals to whom trust has been given but who has lost that trust over time. Tier 3 leaders are under no obligation to trust those who have proven to be untrustworthy. It is important to remember, however, that leaders who begin by trusting others are more likely to build impactful teams than leaders who only trust those who have "earned" their trust in advance or leaders who only trust those who first trust them.

DON'T DELEGATE TASKS: DELEGATE LEADERSHIP AND AUTONOMY

Leaders often use examples of delegation as evidence that they trust their subordinates and operate from the circle of distributed leadership. The general idea behind this feeling is the belief that delegation of any task is an example of trust in action. In this view, the leader would never delegate the task of building the lunchroom schedule or the testing calendar to anyone who was not trusted to do the job and do it well.

Not micromanaging delegated tasks is a concrete example of the actions of a trusting leader. The leader who delegates the task and then trusts the individual or team assigned to complete the task without micromanaging the task sees themselves as a trusting leader.

This ability to delegate tasks and then allow those tasks to be accomplished without micromanaging the people responsible for the delegated task is not, however, Tier 3 trust-building behavior. Effective delegation does require a set of leadership skills, and leaders who delegate effectively are much more likely to be effective managers as well as more likely to have time to dedicate to Tier 2 and Tier 3 behaviors. But effective delegation of routine tasks is not sufficient when attempting to build trust throughout the system.

To "trust down" the organization is not just to delegate tasks, or to refrain from micromanaging the behaviors of those assigned to complete the delegated task, particularly if those tasks are management (Tier 1) tasks.

Delegating management activities does not build or imply trust. In fact, delegating management tasks may be viewed by subordinates as proof that the leader does not have the trust or confidence in the employees to assign meaningful tasks, tasks that may impact the core mission of the organization.

In addition, only delegating management tasks is likely to overwhelm and trap those carrying out those tasks from having the time and resources necessary to work at Tier 2 tasks—as instructional leaders—or at Tier 3 tasks—as interpersonal leaders. In many schools and school districts, even individuals with job descriptions that do come with mission-driven leadership responsibilities cannot be successful because they are trapped in managing so many routine daily activities.

The assistant principal who is spending 90 percent of his time on classroom management or on managing the testing calendar, or the mid-level district leader who is bogged down in managing the myriad state and national reports required—these are just a few examples of how the delegation of tasks is done at the expense of the assignment of meaningful mission objectives.

To keep building genuine two-way trust is to delegate the leadership autonomy and authority necessary to accomplish meaningful components of the overall school mission. It is to delegate Tier 2 and Tier 3 initiatives. It is to delegate not only the task of completing Tier 2 and 3 initiatives, but also to delegate all of the necessary resources and decision-making responsibilities that are needed to complete those missions.

Stakeholders and members of the organization don't feel trusted just because a task has been given to them to complete. In fact, leaders who over-delegate, or who delegate only basic operational tasks, are likely to be viewed by their colleagues as ineffective, selfish, and self-centered. These leaders see themselves as the only ones with the authority and expertise to make the "big" decisions within the organization. These leaders delegate administrative functions to others so they can spend the majority of their time as the sole leader and decision-maker for the important issues the organization faces.

RECOGNIZE THE CONSEQUENCES OF BEGINNING WITH TRUST

Trusting behavior is risky behavior. Just because the leader begins each day by trusting down the organization does not mean that that trust will be rewarded with excellent results, or even compliance by all stakeholders. There is always the possibility that even when given the authority and resources to complete the mission, some trusted subordinates will fail in their efforts, or worse yet, misuse the authority provided to them by the leader. Distributed leadership is, by definition, leadership that involves more and more individuals wielding real decision-making authority. Distributed leadership is not easier than isolated leadership.

The more people there are involved in complex activities, the easier it is to have communication issues, differences of opinion, and lack of standardization. Effective collaboration requires practice, systems to support and train those involved in the process, and ongoing communication about what is working and what is not working. Not everyone on the team has equal levels of commitment to the organization or the tasks at hand, nor do they have equal talent and skills necessary to be high performing.

While distributed leadership is not easier than leading from a position of power and isolation, distributed leadership is more effective at accomplishing complex difficult goals and is more effective at building trust and commitment from throughout the organization. When individuals in the organization prove to be untrustworthy or incapable of committing to the mission and work of the organization, the leader still has the power of the position to respond, as well as the support of the rest of the team.

What can and should the leader do when certain followers betray or don't live up to the trust and responsibility that has been given? Trust must be maintained by all parties in an organization. Of course there is always a risk, a leap of faith, regarding trust and any relationship. Just as leaders can lose the trust of followers, so, too, can leaders lose the trust they have given to followers.

Trust is fragile. Trust needs to be nourished and tended to over time. Building and maintaining trust in any relationship requires daily commitment and ongoing communication. There is always risk. There is greater risk, however, in expecting every follower in the organization to automatically trust the leader.

It is for these reasons that many leaders fear the delegation of any meaningful organizational activity. Many leaders assume that the potential pitfalls of distributed leadership, in which ever-increasing members of the organization are trusted to undertake complex and challenging assignments, are simply too great. In this view, the leader feels it is safer to centralize the decision-making process.

After all, the leader is responsible and accountable for mission success, so the leader should decide and implement the mission strategy. In this leadership view, the followers in the organization are expected to "trust up" the organization, and the structure of decision-making and communication is the vertical pyramid.

If schools were simple organizations, with easily attainable goals, then "trusting up" the organization might work. If schools operated on steady, reliable, and sufficient human and financial resources, then "trusting up" the organization might work. If schools had consistent policy directives and quality control over all stakeholders involved in the process, both internal and external, then "trusting up" the organization might work.

Clearly, none of these organizational descriptions are in place today or will be in place tomorrow. In fact, the opposite is true. Schools are complex. Resources are uncertain. Stakeholders are volatile. Success is ambiguous. The risks of not building organizational cultures in which trust is distributed are far greater than the risks of doing so.

What positive benefits to the culture, climate, and ability to achieve organizational goals occur in systems not based on the pyramid? What does it look like when followers are trusted? As stated, in environments as complex as today's schools, there is no one leader who has the skill set, the expertise, and the time to single-handedly achieve the overarching mission of the school. Effective school leadership in the twenty-first century is a team enterprise. Effective school leaders recognize that the smartest person in the room . . . is the room.

The real risk is not in being a leader who trusts down the organization; the real risk is being a leader who does not trust down the organization. There is a chance that trusting down the organization will not always work. But there is a guarantee that not trusting down the organization will fail. The willingness and the ability to begin each day by trusting others is a prerequisite for leadership success. It is a high impact daily behavior.

TODAY'S TRUST LIST

For a leader to trust down the organization successfully, daily leadership behaviors that model trust and that support distributed leadership must occur. Trust is a fragile commodity. The trust between leaders and followers that can take months and years to build can be damaged or destroyed overnight. Trusting down the organization is more than a philosophy or a leadership orientation; it is a daily activity.

Many leaders use a variety of organizational activities to make sure they accomplish the primary tasks of the day or the week. From completing to-do lists to creating strategic action plans, effective leaders are organized leaders.

Effective leaders understand how to prioritize. Like many interpersonal skills, however, "building and maintaining trust" may not appear at all on the strategic plan, on the to-do list of the leader. What would a "trust list" even look like? What planning, what activities, would make up a strategic plan to build and maintain trust?

Leaders committed to a trusting-down orientation don't just say that they trust the team; they show by their actions that they trust the team. These leaders look at the activities that are being delegated out to teams to make sure that, while there certainly will be, and should be, Tier 1 and Tier 2 activities on the list, there are also significant numbers of important Tier 3 mission activities being delegated.

Each day, leaders who "trust down" delegate responsibilities other than managerial responsibilities. Each day, leaders who "trust down" evaluate the decisions being made, the messages being sent, and the organizational structures in use for the day to make sure that all of those behaviors reflect that of a leader who truly trusts the team. Each day, leaders committed to successfully distributed leadership evaluate the degree to which they are supporting, in word and in action, the teams to whom leadership responsibility has been distributed.

THE TRUSTED FOLLOWER

Of course, all leaders want, and need, the trust of the people who work for them. Teams, by definition, have a common goal. Teams that are high functioning have common characteristics. Leaders committed to the power of teams must also commit to all that goes into developing the team. The development of others must be a top priority for the Tier 3 leader.

The trusted follower must also have expert power. The trusted follower must also have a commitment to the mission. Tier 3 leaders prioritize the activities and behaviors that build expertise and mission understanding for as many stakeholders as possible. Leaders who assign meaningful tasks to teams without providing ongoing support, whether that be training or resources, are not leaders who will succeed. It is not the fault of the team when failure occurs if that team has not been selected, supported, developed, and mentored on an ongoing basis by the leader.

Most leaders recognize the critical importance of trust in any relationship. Every leader needs to be trusted and to have trust in others. Tier 3 leaders, however, also recognize that how that trust is established—under what circumstances and expectations that trust is communicated between the leader and followers—matters even more. Tier 3 leaders work each and every day in ways that demonstrate the trust the leader has in the team. Tier 3 leaders trust down.

TODAY IS A GOOD DAY TO TRUST DOWN

1. Today is a good day to transfer decision-making authority to teachers. Leadership exists at every level of the organization. High-impact leaders take advantage of that deep leadership pool.
2. Today is a good day to think about the actions and messaging that need to occur that will demonstrate trust in all stakeholders. What leaders say is important, but it is what leaders do, and how leaders interact with others, that says the most, and that has the biggest impact, on how stakeholders at all levels of the organization view the leader.
3. Today is a good day to demonstrate trust in student leaders. In many schools, it is the untapped potential of the student leader that is missing. When students take an active and important role in the overall leadership of the organization, student buy-in and belief in the capacity of the school to make a difference increases significantly. Find a school with a great culture and climate, and you will find a school with active, involved students.
4. Today is a good day to make sure leadership actions align with leadership words. Impactful leaders take stock of the actions of the day to ensure that what has been seen by all stakeholders is aligned with what has been heard by all stakeholders.
5. Today is a great day to encourage colleagues and students to be innovative risk takers. The fear of failure is one of the biggest obstacles to innovation. High-performing leaders build cultures that reward innovation and recognize that failure is part of the process whenever big goals are undertaken. Organizations that learn from failure rather than fearing failure are organizations that are likely to make a difference.
6. Today is a great day to trust your team with a big, bold, mission-driven initiative. When leaders trust down the organization with tasks that are significant and are understood as such by everyone in the organization, then a mission-driven, team-oriented culture that includes all stakeholders is likely.
7. Today is a good day to do unto teachers what leaders ask teachers to do unto students. Leaders are often very good at identifying best practice in communication, in team building, and in goal-driven activity between teachers and students. Unfortunately, for many leaders this same ability to recognize the importance of best practice behaviors in communication, team building, and goal development between leaders and teachers is not in place.
8. Today would be a good day to remove all of the doors to your office. Without transparency, there is no lasting trust. One way to ensure that

business is not being conducted behind closed doors is to have as few doors as possible.
9. Today is a good day to make a list of all the ways in which leadership teams working in the organization are being supported. Don't just assume that simply because teams are in place and have been given significant assignments, the work of distributing leadership is done. Without effective ongoing support—both personnel and financial—in place, long-term success is unlikely.

Chapter Ten

Lead Up the Organization

The direction of organizational leadership orientation moving from a vertical pyramidal structure to a team-oriented horizontal circular structure was discussed in depth in chapter 9. Most of the time, for most leaders, the daily orientation of the leader and the leadership team is down through the organization (Pearce & Conger, 2002). Because most leaders operate in organizational hierarchies based on position power, leaders tend to spend a majority of their time thinking about how to motivate, influence, and evaluate those employees who report up to the leader.

It is the leader's job to take all of the stakeholders and employees within the organization and build systems that result in the organization successfully meeting its goals and objectives. Leaders are given position power (discussed in chapter 7) in order to assist the leader in ensuring that subordinates accomplish their assigned tasks and job responsibilities. Leaders tend to think about using their position power so that they can accomplish the organization's goals. Leaders who are well versed in the limitations of position power as a leadership tool will also rely on expert power and mission voice to influence and direct the activities of all of the individuals for whom the leader is responsible.

There is another, more powerful leadership orientation that will impact the success of any leader working to achieve the mission and overarching goals of any organization, though. This leadership orientation cannot rely on position power; it must rely on expert power and the leader's ability to influence those colleagues and superiors who do not report up to the leader.

Often this orientation is focused directly on the members of the organization to whom the leader is reporting, the leader's bosses. Extraordinary leaders see the value in and have the ability to lead and influence their superiors, those to whom they report. In this leadership view, power is actually measured by the ability of the leader to influence others in the organization (Lunenburg, 2012). Tier 3 leaders strive on a daily basis not only to lead down the organization, but also to lead, to influence, up the organization.

LEAD UP

This "leading up" orientation is purposeful on the part of the high-performing leader. Leading up does not happen by accident. Leaders have specific goals they wish to accomplish. Specific strategies are used by the leader when working with organizational superiors to accomplish those goals. These strategies include building formal networks, volunteering for assignments that impact the organization beyond the leader's current assignment, modeling and sharing successful innovations, and developing specific project proposals for consideration by the larger organization (Colwell, 2015).

This orientation requires a paradigm shift in how the leader sees the leader's role in the overall organization. This leadership mind-set requires the leader to see influence as a two-way street, moving both up and down the organization's leadership structure. This leadership mind-set requires the leader to see that one of the most powerful and effective skills any leader can possess, regardless of their job description or formal place on the organization's hierarchy, is the ability to influence all stakeholders regardless of their position in the system.

In a very fundamental way, high-impact leadership—leadership that makes a difference, that is sustainable over time—is about the ability to influence others (Pink, 2014). The ability to successfully influence those to whom the leader reports is just as important, if not more so, than the ability to influence those who report to the leader. It takes strong leadership skills to motivate and influence those in the organization who report to the leader. It takes real leadership expertise at the highest levels, however, to motivate and influence those in the organization who reside above the leader in the organizational hierarchy.

Recognizing that influencing up the organization is just as important and effective of a leadership skill as influencing down the organization is an important first step for any leader working to make a significant impact on their organization. Committing to learning and using specific strategies that will improve the thinking and actions of those to whom the leader reports can be challenging and time consuming.

Clearly, leading any constituency is challenging in the complex world of teaching and learning, and leading those with more power than yourself is harder than leading your own team. There is no Tier 1 position power available in any situation when attempting to lead up. Leaders who lead up have no position power, only expert power and interpersonal skill/mission voice power. The skills and strategies that work, however, when leading peers and subordinates, strategies that do not rely at all on position power, will also work when applied to those in the organization with more position power.

EXPAND THE CIRCLE

Careers spent in classrooms, schools, and school districts are, by their nature, often isolating professions. The classroom teacher closes the door to the room and works alone with the students. The assistant principal or principal works long hours in the school, often isolated in an office, never really venturing out to other schools. The district administrator is consumed by responsibilities within the district, rarely visiting other districts except for meetings with agendas already established by someone else for someone else's purpose.

In each of these cases, the danger of becoming both physically and intellectually isolated from what is happening—outside the classroom for the teacher, outside the school for the school leader, and outside the district for the district administrator—is real and limiting.

Often without even thinking about how the day is spent and whom the day is spent with, educators at all levels of the organization can find themselves networking only with the stakeholders inside the organization they lead and at the level in which they work, or not networking with anyone at all.

High-impact leaders, however, recognize the value in building formal networks with other educators who work outside of the leader's formal scope of responsibilities (Pearce, 2007). These formal networks are more than the random informal discussions that might occur at chance meetings or even at meetings called by superiors to present information or discuss issues of the day.

While there is great value in the communication and information sharing that can occur when principals get together for a monthly meeting, or any gathering of educators for a specific purpose, these meetings, by their very nature, are typically not designed for networking and are not organized by the leaders involved in the meetings, but by leaders with more position power who have an agenda of their own.

Formal networking structures should be built by leaders at every level of the organization. These networks will not only serve as an effective strategy to improve performance, but they will also assist the leader in leading up the organization. High-impact leaders take the time to build and participate in these networks. These formal networks can and should consist of two distinct membership types: job-alike networks and vertical networks. There is great value in building, or joining, networks of individuals with similar job duties and responsibilities, job-alike networks, and networks made up of individuals from all levels of the organization (Pearce, 2007).

BUILD JOB-ALIKE NETWORKS

Job-alike networks consist of individuals with common job responsibilities, challenges, and opportunities. When elementary-school principals can communicate in environments that are safe, where trust has been established, with other elementary-school principals, there is a great opportunity to both learn new strategies and avoid common mistakes. Job-alike formal networks can exist at any level of the organization, from first-year assistant principal networks to networks of district superintendents.

The opportunity to influence other leaders, serving in the same capacity, by sharing what is working and what is not working, by brainstorming and organizing strategically around a common mission or a common set of problems, is there for any leader who seeks to improve the quality of their own leadership or to influence the organization on a larger scale. Leaders who are active in job-alike networks are "leading out." These leaders are able to influence, and be influenced, by other leaders working on the same goals and objectives.

Wherever an individual resides in the organization's hierarchy, there is a need to network, to learn from others in the same position and to share what has been learned with others. Organized job-alike networking can be a valuable use of a leader's time. It is important, as well, for leaders to allow others within the organization to participate in job-alike and vertical networks. Too many leaders network themselves, but they do not build the time for networking into the schedules of their subordinates. Tier 3 leaders not only allow everyone on the team to network, but they also expect networking to play a vital role in the development of the team as a whole and of the individuals who make up the team.

BUILD VERTICAL NETWORKS

Unlike job-alike networks, vertical networks consist of colleagues and stakeholders who are working in jobs with less position power and/or with more position power. Teacher leaders, school-based leaders, and district leaders can and should build formal networks together. By working with colleagues from all levels of the organization, leaders increase their ability to influence all levels of the organization and increase their understanding of how the organization is functioning at all levels.

Fundamental questions can be addressed though formal vertical networks: What are the issues other colleagues face? How they are the same, and how are they different, from the issues being faced at the leader's level? How does the behavior of the leader impact these other levels within the organization?

All of these questions, and the ability to deepen an understanding of the impact of leader decisions on those above and below in the organization are enhanced when leaders take the opportunity to build formal, ongoing vertical networks. There are opportunities for leaders to volunteer for vertical networks that are already in place; there are also opportunities for leaders to form their own vertical networks.

Leaders cannot have expert power about organizational functions, challenges, and successes for those working below the leader if the leader never interacts, in formal and purposeful ways, with those who report to the leader. It is just as true that leaders cannot influence up the organization if the leader is never interacting with members of the organization who reside higher up the food chain. Leaders who are involved in vertical networks are also more likely to build consensus throughout the organization as a result of the collaboration and teamwork that can occur though these networks.

VOLUNTEER

Volunteer for duties and responsibilities beyond your current assignment. Perhaps the simplest and easiest way for leaders to begin to "lead up" the organization is to volunteer for committees, task forces, or assignments that are outside the normal scope of their own job descriptions. Most leaders remain completely focused on implementing the responsibilities that come with the job. High-impact leaders, however—leaders with a "leading up" orientation—recognize that moving beyond the scope of the job is what leaders who are working to influence the organization as a whole need to do.

Meeting all of the job requirements for any school leader in this complex age of schooling is, in and of itself, a challenge. It can seem counterintuitive to deliberately add more job responsibilities onto the leader's plate when it can be easily argued that there are not enough resources, and not enough time, to complete the tasks in the existing job descriptions with fidelity. While there are challenges involved in adding to the scope of the existing job descriptions, however, there are also multiple benefits to becoming active in the larger scope of the organization.

IT'S ABOUT TIME

Too many leaders use the reality of limited resources and limited time to explain why they are stuck at Tier 1 management tasks all day, working more as reactive firefighters than proactive mission builders. The lack of time is the reason they never reach Tier 2 expert power behavior or Tier 3 interpersonal team-building behavior.

What may appear counterintuitive to leaders with this "there is just no time" mind-set is the fact that the skills learned, the contacts and partnerships gained, and the mission benefits realized from interacting with and impacting those above the leader in the organization, or outside of the organization, far outweigh the challenges of organizing and prioritizing the limited resources and hours in the day that are available to all leaders.

First, the leader who volunteers for work outside the scope of the job description will learn and increase expert power through this process. Leaders who have been in the same job for many years can easily fall into the trap of believing that they have seen it all and know it all. By expanding job responsibilities through volunteering, the leader is placed into new situations with new goals and objectives that require new skill sets or levels of expertise. By expanding job expertise through designing projects or recommending solutions for projects not currently under the responsibility of the leader, additional expert power will result.

Leaders who volunteer to serve in capacities outside of their normal job scope and leaders who design solutions for superiors to consider are leaders who are learning and increasing expert power. Leaders who are learning are leaders who can sustain leadership over time.

IT'S ABOUT INFLUENCE

Second, the leader who volunteers to serve on committees outside of the normal job scope or who proposes solutions for problems not directly tied to the leader's job demonstrates the ability to impact the organization in a variety of settings and on a variety of projects. As discussed earlier, leadership is primarily a function of the ability to influence others. High-impact leaders are role models. There is a direct correlation between the degree of authenticity that a leader demonstrates through word and deed and the authenticity of the commitment of followers to demonstrate the same behaviors (Gardner, Avolio, et al., 2005).

The leader's capacity to influence others grows as more members of the organization, including those who may have a higher position in the organization, see the leader at work in settings outside the normal scope of their job duties. Leaders who volunteer are obviously being proactive, and they are seen that way by superiors.

With so many obvious benefits to being a leader who is actively volunteering for school- and-district based assignments, why do so few leaders utilize this strategy? As mentioned earlier, the simplest and most common answer is the leader's belief that there simply is not enough time in the day to take on additional tasks. For most leaders, the workday—the entire workweek—is already overloaded with too many meetings, too many tasks to accomplish. Adding even more onto the leader's plate seems not only impossible, but foolhardy.

How can the leader justify spending less time on campus or in the office, when there already feels like insufficient time to accomplish the goals and objectives that are already on the leader's to-do list? Won't the leader have to delegate even more responsibilities to others in the organization, who themselves are also overwhelmed with the scope of the job?

The leadership dilemma regarding the lack of time is the "go to" excuse for not only this Tier 3 leadership strategy, but for many, if not most of the strategies discussed throughout this book. Too many leaders who are stuck at Tier 1 or Tier 2 are stuck there because time controls the behavior of the leader rather than the leader controlling how time is prioritized and used.

The irony is that by letting time become the driving variable in determining what a leader does, rather than by letting mission and impact determine how the leader spends time, the time-controlled leader becomes less successful, less impactful, and less likely to make a profound difference within the organization.

Obviously time is a fixed variable. How time is used by leaders, however, can vary widely. How tasks are prioritized, and how decisions are made to increase the number of leaders within the organization—by trusting down the organization, by reducing position power, by dancing with the dancers, and by leading as an interpersonal expert—is what separates Tier 3 leaders from Tier 1 and Tier 2 leaders.

Tier 3 leaders don't create time to volunteer or engage in these mission-driven behaviors; they prioritize the time needed to focus on impact behaviors. Tier 3 leaders don't create time so that they can accomplish even more tasks; they create additional leaders by increasing the number and quality of the leadership team that is engaged and empowered to complete the work.

SUCCESS LOVES COMPANY

Tier 3 leaders model and share successful innovations. Success loves company. Everyone typically begins their work in the organization wanting to make a difference, to be successful. This is true of the first-year teacher, the first-year assistant principal, and the first-year superintendent of schools. Even colleagues who appear disengaged or hostile to the work are typically just behaving out of boredom or frustration.

In this view, burnout is more a function of attitude toward the job, and experiences on the job, rather than years on the job. Once engaged and empowered to complete meaningful work, no matter how small, the vast majority of these disengaged coworkers will reengage with the organization and the organization's goals at some level.

Time and time again, examples of small projects, pilot programs, and innovations occurring in just one classroom or just one school become known to the larger education community. Tier 3 leaders are supporting these innovations through the distributed leadership strategies discussed throughout this book. Tier 3 leaders are aware of these innovations and spread the word about these small, but successful projects.

Early adopters, the dancers, will then join the movement and spread the innovation by joining in on the practice. Mission-driven leaders provide support, perhaps some small amount of financial aid, some small amount of time needed to plan or implement the innovation, or encouragement to stakeholders to take risks and strive for a better way to meet the organization's goals. Quickly these innovations that began on a small scale generate results that can be measured and shared in formal settings with other leaders throughout the organization.

When those results are successful, the high-impact leader has an opportunity, even an obligation, to share those results with the larger community. It can be as simple as inviting superiors or influential stakeholders to visit and see the innovation in practice. Leading up can be as simple as connecting those innovators, those dancers, to the larger community.

Not only does this strategy allow the innovation to spread and support more classrooms and more schools in their work, it also provides an opportunity for the leader to recognize the accomplishments of the innovators on a larger stage. What educators value most, what provides them with the most job satisfaction, is the knowledge that their work has an impact, that a difference is being made. Sharing the impact of small innovations, of new ideas, with the larger community is highly motivating.

Success loves company. High-impact leaders recognize that when innovation that works is shared, those higher up in the organization will naturally want to share and spread that success throughout the organization, and to the community at large.

INNOVATE

Leaders with a leading-up orientation are the leaders who are developing specific project proposals that impact the larger organization. Leaders at the highest levels of most organizations want and value this innovation and recognize the positive benefits that occur for the organization if a culture that fosters innovation has been developed (Barsh, Capozzi, & Davidson, 2008).

Impact leaders are proactive. Just like every principal has some subset of the faculty that includes the early adopters and innovators, every district has school-based assistant principals and principals who are also early adopters and innovators. When teachers lead up they can influence school-based administrators to get better. Leading-up teachers demonstrate new pedagogical approaches to anyone who will listen. When school administrators lead up, they can influence other schools within the district—and the district itself—toward continuous improvement in the same way.

In short, leaders with a leading-up orientation are the dancers within the administrative ranks. They are the early adopters among the larger set of all individuals who hold leadership positions throughout the organization. A simple, yet highly effective way to be proactive is to develop specific proposals and submit those proposals up the organization's food chain for consideration.

These proposals do not need to be large in scale. These proposals do not need to transform the organization in profound ways or initiate major shifts in the organization's mission or philosophy.

In fact, it is probably an overreach to attempt to lead up via large-scale, complex, time-consuming, and expensive mission proposals. Instead, proposing pilot projects and volunteering to implement them, or proposing that projects that have already been successful on a small scale be tried in more settings or on an incrementally larger scale, are excellent ways to lead up the organization.

Often these proposals to initiate something new and innovative can be piloted right in the leader's classroom or school, and they may already be part of the leader's job responsibilities. For example, the leader may discover a new way of looking at remediating students who are struggling with academic content. The leader's new proposal requires minimal changes in the status quo, and these changes could be tested on a small scale with limited financial or time commitments.

What is needed for the leader to move forward, to influence up the organization, are three things: the will of the leader and of the implementation team to innovate; a strategic plan that clearly outlines the objectives and the action steps needed to reach those objectives; and permission to proceed.

Leading up requires that both the leader and the team see the value of influence as a leadership trait. It requires the leader and team to be thoughtful risk takers, to be able to conceptualize and plan better ways to reach the organization's mission, and to tolerate the risks associated with trying something new, including the risk of failure. When the leader and the leadership team have a leading-up orientation, combined with a willingness to take appropriate risks and try out new ways to reach the organization's mission, the impact of that leadership team will be felt throughout the system.

Chapter 10
LEAD BY BEING LED

Build the capacity for subordinates to influence you. If leaders are going to lead up the organization and have an orientation and focus that is designed to influence those to whom they report, it is important for those same leaders to have a mind-set that accepts influence and direction from their own subordinates. In other words, it is important for the leader also to be a follower, a listener.

Too many people see leadership as centered on authority and position power. These individuals see the primary role of the leader as deciding and delegating to others (Cain, 2017). These leaders have a one-way, downward orientation to leadership. These leaders do not recognize that one of the values and qualities that make up a good follower is the ability to impact the leader. It is important not only for the leaders to see themselves as influencers, but also for leaders to see those who report to them as influencers, as well.

Influence and leading must be seen not as a *one-way* street, always moving from the top of the organization down through the organization, but as a *two-way* street, with every leader, no matter where they are in the organization's hierarchy, willing and able both to influence others and to be influenced by others. Leaders who recognize the power of mentoring others, and of being mentored by others, are leaders who will grow their own leadership capacity and the capacity of others (Browne-Ferrigno & Muth, 2004).

By building relationships and structures, that allow subordinates within the organization or stakeholders from outside the organization to influence leadership behavior, the leader learns the benefits of being influenced as opposed to being just an influencer. Leaders who are open to new ideas, regardless of who originated those ideas, will see a variety of positive changes in the climate, culture, and communication within the organization. When all stakeholders feel that their voices are being heard, when stakeholders realize they have the ability to make a difference within the organization, morale and "buy-in" to the organization's mission goes up.

Isolation is the enemy of effective leadership. Avoiding leadership isolation is more than just making sure that the leader is visible; it also includes the ability to build relationships and organizational structures that allow and encourage everyone in the organization to participate.

If the smartest person in the room, is the room, then innovation and progress will occur only by letting more people into the room and allowing them to wield power through their ability to influence the goals and activities of the organization. If modern school environments are volatile, uncertain, complex, and ambiguous, then only by unleashing the brainpower of everyone in the organization can the leader reasonably expect to reach the organization's goals.

The more successful the leader is in accomplishing the mission, the more influence that leader will have when attempting to guide and influence those to whom they report. Leaders who are open to being influenced, to being led, are more likely to be successful. Leaders with a proven track record of innovation and success are more likely to be heard by their superiors. Leaders who know firsthand the value of being influenced are more likely to recognize the value they bring to the larger organization by having a "leading up" mentality themselves.

Even when the proposed innovation to superiors is occurring on a small scale, the ability of the leader to articulate the need for the proposed changes, and to demonstrate how those changes actually work in the field, increases the likelihood of superiors' acting on the recommendations.

Having a leading-up orientation requires a specific mind-set, as discussed in detail in this chapter. However, leading up, and being led by others who are themselves leading up also, requires a daily commitment to the work needed in order to lead up. Leading up is a mind-set, an orientation, but it is primarily about action. It is about action that occurs on a daily basis, action that is prioritized so that it does, in fact, occur.

TODAY IS A GOOD DAY TO LEAD UP

1. Today is a good day to influence the people to whom the leader reports. The ability to influence others is a key leadership skill. That influence is not limited to those below the leader. Time spent influencing and impacting superiors is also time well spent.
2. Today is a good day to start a new project. High-performing leaders are proactive leaders. Find a new project, even a small one, that will help the organization achieve its goals. Begin planning for the development and implementation of that project today.
3. Today is a good day to share the results of the team with superiors. Leaders at every level of the organization want to know the good news, the success stories, that are occurring out in the field. Letting supervisors know what is being accomplished not only lets the leader share the accomplishments of the team, but it also educates those above the leader about what is working.
4. Today is a good day to join an existing network or to start a new network of educators with a common mission and passion. Leadership is fundamentally all about relationships, and relationships are fundamentally improved when teams of like-minded individuals work together. Networking with existing teams or building new teams with a common mission should be a high-priority leadership activity.

5. Today is a good day to volunteer to serve on a district-level or a state-level committee. One of the best ways to influence up the organization is to join committees, or work groups, that are working on projects whose scope is larger than the leader's current job responsibilities. Not only does this enhance the leader's ability to influence others, but it also increases the leader's expert power.
6. Today is a good day to start an interdisciplinary network of educators on a common mission. Tier 3 leaders don't just join existing networks; they also create new networks of individuals from across the spectrum of the organization.
7. Today is a good day to be open to being influenced by others. It is just as important to be open to being influenced by others as it is to be an influencer. Impactful leaders recognize that leadership skill and capacity exist at all levels of the system and are thus open to being influenced by those leaders wherever they reside in the organization.
8. Today is a good day to ask a colleague to collaborate on a project. Collaboration involves much more than delegating a task; it is a cooperative venture in which all parties work together as equals.
9. Today is a good day to think about how superiors could improve their performance. Most leaders tend to think only about the performance of those who report to them and how to assist, mentor, and coach those colleagues so that their performance improves. However, Tier 3 leaders also do the same thing when thinking about their superiors in the organization.

Chapter Eleven

Focus on Process

Educators live in a world of hyperaccountability. At all levels, from the first-year classroom teacher to the district superintendent, the pressure to meet specific, measurable benchmarks in what feels like a never-ending list of goals to achieve has been expanding for the last thirty years. Teacher evaluations, student grade level promotion and graduation rates, discipline and safety data, standardized test data, and school grades are just a small sample of the educational outcomes that are used to assess teaching, learning, and leadership quality.

This focus on school quality is not new, although it is important to note that for most of our history, the struggle to ensure access to education for all students, regardless of race or background, was a more dominant factor in measuring education progress. For most of the twentieth century, society and policymakers granted educators significant authority to monitor and determine teaching and learning quality. The use of standardized tests was limited compared to today, and when used, had as its primary purpose the formative measurement of student learning as opposed to the summative measurement of teacher quality.

Impactful geopolitical and economic events, such as the Soviet Union's successful launch of the *Sputnik* satellite in the late 1950s, however, began a movement that focused policymakers more on student learning outcomes than on access and equity for all. The Soviets' ability to place a satellite in orbit at a time when the United States attempts at space flight were routinely resulting in failure was seen by many as a clear indication that our education system was not producing competitive graduates.

Serious questions about how school program quality and accountability were monitored and assessed were asked. Were American students falling behind in mathematics and the sciences when measured against the communist bloc nations? Had our curriculum and teaching standards become too soft, too child centered, with not enough academic rigor? Questions like these and the concerns they raised over how to ensure educational quality and accountability slowly but surely grew over the ensuing decades.

The highly publicized and controversial report *A Nation at Risk*, produced in the 1980s, only added to the perception that America's schools were substandard. This time it was not Russia and its threat of communism but Japan and its accompanying economic threat that was seen as a direct threat to the notion of America's dominance in the manufacturing sector and as the unquestioned world economic powerhouse.

Statements like, "If a foreign nation did to America's children what our education system is doing to America's children, we would consider it an act of war" (*A Nation at Risk*, 1984) accelerated the country's move toward a highly regulated and outcome-driven system. The notion that our educational system was failing and badly in need of systemic reform became chiseled into most state school system designs by legislators eager to fix the problem.

With programs such as No Child Left Behind adding the weight of the federal government behind the assessment and accountability movement, today's educators at every level are subject to a barrage of accountability assessments designed to measure quality of system outputs.

Clearly, all leaders need to be focused on what it is that is being measured, how it is being measured, and what needs to be accomplished in order to meet those targets. If the leader doesn't know what success looks like, as defined by school policymakers, they will never know whether or not they are making progress toward it. If the leader doesn't know what the organization's goals are, the leader will not know what to measure, and the leader will not be able to share the purpose of the organization with internal and external stakeholders.

The issue of being goal oriented, what this author refers to as being "mission driven," is fundamentally important for effective leadership. Zenger and Folkman (2009) identify a focus on results as one of the six most important leadership attributes for high-performing leaders in any field. When the leader doesn't understand the organization's ultimate purpose and what outcomes will demonstrate that that purpose is being achieved, the leader doesn't know what to measure, or worse, cannot differentiate between what measurements are worth attending to and what measurements are just background noise resulting in the leader directing the organization's resources and efforts away from the primary mission.

BEGIN WITH THE PROCESS IN MIND

Having a strong focus on results is a *necessary* leadership mind-set. However, focusing on results is not a *sufficient* leadership mind-set. Too often school leaders become fixated on the product, the goal they are trying to reach, at the expense of the time and thoughtfulness needed to focus on the processes that lead to those desired results. While it is true that all high-performing leaders must focus on the desired results of the organization (Zenger, Folkman, 2009), it is the focus on the process itself, rather than a focus on the outcome, that is most likely to get the organization to those desired results.

In addition to beginning with the end in mind, Tier 3 leaders must also begin with the process in mind. Tier 3 leaders recognize that leadership involves more than working with people, it also requires working with and leading systems (Avolio, 1999).

Ultimately, effective leadership in the modern age involves the ability of the leader to be an expert problem solver, and more importantly, to be able to understand which problems and which processes, which systems, associated with those problems are impacting the overall culture of the school (Leithwood, Begley, & Cousins, 2005).

Once clear, measurable goals and outcomes have been established and agreed upon by all stakeholders, the high-performing leader moves toward process design. The leadership orientation then becomes about how the work needed to achieve the goals will be accomplished and how progress will be measured. The evaluation of all of the implementation processes become formative rather than summative, with a focus on evaluating the quality and success of the process itself as opposed to only evaluating the end results of the process. It is a leadership mistake to obsess about program goals and minimize the attention paid to the program's processes and systems that have been designed to reach those goals.

BUILD SYSTEMS TO GET FORMATIVE FEEDBACK

Too often, educators, at all levels, wait for the final test results, the state end-of-year report, or some other summative assessment before validating the quality of the year's work and the strategies that were used to reach organization goals. It is not that summative reports don't have value or that the results from summative assessments can't be used strategically to make the organization better.

These summative reports have clear value. Just as doctors can learn from the results of an autopsy, so, too, can educators learn a great deal from data that summarizes a project's status at the end of the mission. Autopsies can help doctors understand the correlation between smoking and lung cancer or assist in determining a specific cause of death. This information can be shared with other doctors and the patients they serve as valuable information moving forward.

A summative analysis of educational data about students at the end of a grading term, at the close of a school year, or at the conclusion of a high-stakes standardized test can also reveal important causal information that can lead to program improvements for the next cohort of students.

No one in the medical field, however, would argue that the health-care system should rely only on autopsy data to determine the overall quality of the medical care being delivered or the overall health of the living. Likewise, no one in the education field should rely only on summative data to determine the quality of teaching and learning or the overall academic health of students. Summative data is, by its very nature, only valuable for understanding what to do next time; there is no value in the autopsy for the body undergoing the procedure.

Formative data, data that is gathered during the process, must be used to improve and monitor program quality. The annual physical exam is designed to produce results for the patient being examined. Formative evaluations of school system processes and outcomes are also valuable in determining mid-course corrections for students and teachers. Impact leaders can use this data to evaluate and measure the quality of the systems that are in place to reach the organization's goals.

CAST A WIDE NET

The formative monitoring systems used by high-performing leaders interested in improving outcomes by improving processes must also include data, information, input, and honest feedback from all stakeholders in the organization, as well as from critical allies outside the organization. Where leaders gather their formative data is just as important as what data is being collected. For leaders operating in tight vertical pyramidal structures with tightly controlled lines of communication, the number of individuals providing feedback to the leader can be very limited.

In this case, upper-level management may feel that program implementation and overall efficacy is going quite well, but they lack vital information, because important segments of the organization's employees are not being asked to provide feedback or status reports at all.

When leaders operate from a flat circle and communication system, when they cast a wide net by seeking information from a wide variety of stakeholders, however, the likelihood of having a clearer understanding of process quality goes up. It is not a question of getting more information to the leaders and leadership team from a few individuals; it is a question of getting the right information to the leadership team from a range of individuals throughout the system.

HONESTY IS THE BEST POLICY

High-performing leaders build systems that honestly assess the progress of the work. Simply knowing that formative systems must involve all stakeholders is not enough. Leaders and all stakeholders must also use specific communication structures designed to honestly and transparently assess all systems in the organization. When schools and school districts are led by teams of people committed to open, honest assessment of the quality of all programs, these programs will improve. It is not just that what gets measured gets done. It is that what gets measured accurately and reported in an honest and transparent manner gets done well.

The systems designed to ensure program process quality should meet several criteria. First, these systems should be designed and vetted by a wide cross section of the education community. Systems designed to gather open and honest feedback about program quality that themselves have not been designed through an open and honest process are unlikely to inspire trust or understanding. Tier 3 leaders use the strategies discussed in this book, strategies like trusting down the organization, dancing with the dancers, and using mission and expert power to strategically plan how to monitor the organization itself.

Second, these systems should operate in the sunshine. Process monitoring not only needs to be designed in a transparent way, but the system itself needs to operate, on a daily basis, in a transparent way. If the process designed to monitor program quality and implement programmatic changes is done by a small group of individuals with position power behind closed doors, even if those processes are being implemented as designed, it is inevitable that questions regarding the process will arise. Secrecy does not build efficiency; secrecy destroys trust.

Finally, the processes built by the organization, and implemented in a public and transparent way, should also include clear procedures for revising the process framework itself. Over time, as the organization grows and changes, as new leaders and followers emerge, and as new outcomes are identified, there will be a need for review processes that have been built and also undergo periodic review.

For example, what educators know about pedagogy in 2017—how to measure quality teaching and develop quality teachers—is far more sophisticated and thorough than what was known on the same subject thirty years ago. Therefore, the processes leaders use to assess teacher quality and plan professional development and continuous improvement opportunities for teachers must also have built-in components that allow the system itself to evolve.

LET THE OUTSIDE IN

Tier 3 leaders build and support external review teams to also review and provide advice on the progress of the organization toward meeting its goals. It is human nature to become so embedded in the details of one's own work that processes, systems, and issues that might seem obvious to someone new on the team or someone from outside the system remain completely invisible and unrecognized by the leader or leadership team. This inability to not see the forest for the trees can occur at any level of the organization.

Teachers who truly believe that they are holding their students to a high level of academic rigor may not see that, in fact, they have lowered student expectations when compared with other teachers in the school or the field. School-based leaders who believe that they are spending 50 percent or more of their time on Tier 2 and Tier 3 leadership tasks may, in fact, be falling far short of that standard.

Strategies such as utilizing peer review systems or external review teams who are focused on assisting the organization in their efforts for continuous improvement can be beneficial in helping the organization take a fresh look at system processes. By inviting stakeholders from outside the organization to formatively assess the organization's goals, processes, and outcomes, the leaders of the organization are also modeling transparency and trust in both the members of the organization and the public as a whole.

Building external review teams means much more than cooperating with, or participating in, state and national site visits from accreditation teams, which often only occur every five or six years.

LET THE PEERS IN

To assess and impact system processes, Tier 3 leaders use peer review and external stakeholder review as an ongoing and regularly scheduled process. This combination of peer reviews and stakeholder reviews causes formative process evaluations to be very helpful. Peer review teams—teams made up of educators serving in similar capacities—have a built-in understanding of the organization's mission, the academic language of the organization, and the organizational constraints typically faced. In addition, these peer review teams can easily operate as formative evaluators.

Peer reviews, when structured with their purpose clearly understood by everyone involved, can be much less threatening than external teams sent by the district, state, or a national accrediting body. As peers, the visiting individual or team hold no position power authority over the system they are evaluating; the team is functioning specifically as a critical friend, another set of expert eyes.

Ongoing external review does not need to be laborious and time consuming for either the vising team (individual) or the school site being assessed. While it is certainly valuable to have an ongoing system of comprehensive system and outcome reviews, smaller targeted visits looking at very specific aspects of the organization can be just as valuable and easier and quicker to implement and sustain.

A school principal for a large and comprehensive high school, for example, asked a peer from another district to come onto the campus once a semester. The reviewer's goal was simple. The task: Visit classrooms and common areas of the campus, then make a list of the first ten impressions, good or bad, that the visitor had about the school. These impressions might be as simple as how the individual was greeted at the front desk, the impression that the school grounds gave regarding cleanliness, or a specific pedagogical impression gathered from classroom walk-throughs.

More focused external reviews can be developed that target specific academic programs or school operational systems. Invite a team of school counselors to observe and provide formative feedback on the school's guidance and counseling system. Ask advanced placement teachers to review course syllabi and assessments. Invite subject area specialists, athletic directors, and security experts to visit and make recommendations.

Just as students in class who are working with teachers who have an open-door policy quickly become used to having classroom visits, so, too, can entire school faculties and school communities easily learn to value and grow comfortable working in an environment that uses a comprehensive system of external peer evaluation.

Not only do Tier 3 leaders recognize the many benefits gained from opening their campus and organization to formative assessments from peers and other interested outside parties, they recognize the value of also serving as a peer assessor for other institutions.

Any leader who has had the opportunity to serve on a site review team, or even an informal site visit to another school or district, recognizes that often the observer learns as much from the visit as those being visited. Any leader who has the opportunity to visit and interact with peers also recognizes the value of networking and building a cohort of like-minded leaders that can result from this type of interaction.

SEE THE CHANGES

Tier 3 leaders are not afraid to change and make mid-course corrections. They are also, however, not afraid to stay the course. There are countless expressions in our popular vernacular that deal with both staying too long on any particular mission or on abandoning promising practices too quickly. Everyone is familiar with statements like, "Don't chase good money after bad money," or "Don't throw the baby out with the bathwater," or "He can't see the forest for the trees," and on and on.

Perhaps one of the toughest decisions a leader can make is to know when is the appropriate time to stop, to change direction, to know when to say when. In many leadership cultures, leaders wait far too long before changing course. Many organizational cultures fear and avoid change and the change process altogether (Evans, 1996). As a result, the school or the district often find themselves doing the same thing year after year with the same system processes in use, resulting in the same outcomes with no systems plan to assess what is not working or design what might be improved.

Managing school discipline, and other school climate processes, are often examples of systems using the same strategies and earning the same results year after year with no significant improvement in outcome. Most adults who have been out of schools for decades would quickly recognize the classroom management systems in place in most schools today.

That is not to say that just because systems are unchanged over extended periods of time that they are arcane. If program goals are being met, assessment targets are being reached, and customer satisfaction is high, there may be no need for change. For many institutions, however, large and small, none of those program and process outcomes are in place, yet the various systems remain unchanged.

The opposite error can also occur when leaders make significant changes in program strategies or even program goals too quickly. It has been this author's experience that, in many schools, innovation and promising practices are quickly abandoned if early data is not promising. It sometimes feels like the cemetery of education innovation is filled with infant graves, with projects that might last one or two years and then are quickly abandoned if initial outcome data do not immediately meet expectations.

As a result, educators at all levels find themselves in the middle of what feels like a never-ending wave of new and improved educational reform movements. Since no project or goal has any sense of permanence or strategic long-term planning behind it, many education cultures become filled with stakeholders who see no value in committing their time or their heart toward any mission. Why should stakeholders commit to challenging work if the work itself will change as soon as a new principal or a new set of laws and regulations appear?

While leaders must be results oriented and have a clear understanding of what success looks like and what measures and outcomes are needed in order to move the organization forward, an even more important orientation is a leadership focus on process, for it is only through the systems that a leader's team designs that those organizational goals will be met.

Continuous improvement occurs when the processes designed and used to assess all aspects of program quality are in place. Continuous improvement occurs when those processes have been built by a wide group of stakeholders and vetted openly throughout the organization. Continuous improvement occurs when those processes also operate in the sunshine so all stakeholders can see directly that agreed-upon systems for program and personnel assessment are in use. For all of these reasons, a daily focus on process is a high-impact Tier 3 leadership behavior.

TODAY IS A GOOD DAY TO FOCUS ON PROCESS

1. Today is a good day to attend a partnership meeting typically delegated to some other member of the leadership team. Leaders who remain visible and active at every level of the organization are seen as more approachable and more knowledgeable than leaders who remain isolated. Time spent meeting with colleagues and stakeholders is time well spent.
2. Today is a good day to review your formative assessment process for evaluating student progress. In an era that relies heavily on summative standardized testing to assess the quality of student learning, the need to have formative assessment systems that cover all aspects of what it means to be "well educated" are more important than ever.
3. Today is a good day to update the processes in place for providing professional development support to the faculty. Building the capacity of others is a fundamental leadership task. When expert power increases across the team, performance increases.
4. Today is a good day to look at processes that lead to team-oriented decision-making. By reviewing the decision-making processes that are actually occurring on a daily basis, the leader can get a clearer picture of the degree to which those processes are open and transparent, or are closed and opaque. When leaders have a clear understanding of how decisions are being made and who has input into the decision-making process, the leader can begin to build more team input into the overall process.
5. Today is a good day to ask students what matters most to them. There is no stakeholder more important in education than the student. It is the support of the student that drives the mission of the organization.

Tier 3 leaders recognize that communicating in significant and ongoing ways with the student body of the school or school district is a critical prerequisite to having a positive organizational culture and climate.

6. Today is a good day to make a list of all the experts in your organization. Expert power resides at all levels of the organization. Taking the time to locate those experts and seek out the guidance and counsel of those individuals is time well spent. Too many leaders seek counsel from the same limited number of individuals in the organization.
7. Today is a good day to talk to colleagues about what you are interested in knowing more about. Leaders who are interested, who inquire, are leaders who are learning. When leaders are perceived by others as lifelong learners, those same leaders are perceived by others as having expert power.
8. Today is a good day to start a "creativity conversation." Creativity is at or near the top of the most desired worker attributes sought out by Fortune 500 companies. It is easy for education systems to get caught up in developing student basic knowledge (the lower levels of Bloom's taxonomy) at the expense of creativity and critical thinking. The same thing can happen to adults in the system. Teamwork, mission-building activity, and strategic planning can all fall victim to a lack of creative thinking. High-performing leaders work each day to support creative thinking.
9. Today is a good day to talk about why specific mission targets exist and whether those targets are the correct ones. Too many leaders take for granted that what is getting measured, and has been measured for years or decades before, are the correct measurement targets for organizational success. Leaders who not only evaluate the processes that are in place to achieve the system's goals, but also evaluate the goals themselves are more likely to build systems that remain current and relevant in a rapidly changing world.
10. Today is a good day to remind stakeholders that the work has value and will make a difference. In every organization, at every level, the daily grind of the work and the many management tasks associated with the work can begin to diminish the importance and the impact that the job has on making a difference in the lives of students. Everyone needs to be reminded of the big picture, the overall reason for the work in the first place. Too often, those reasons are taken for granted.

Chapter Twelve

Dance with the Dancers

Every organization has early adopters, those colleagues ready and willing to try new initiatives or pilot new and innovative ways to impact the organization. These colleagues or stakeholders are the organization's "first followers." There is a common set of behaviors that unites these individuals and is uniquely valuable to the overall success of the organization.

These dancers are typically mission driven. They want to get better at what they do; they want to see the results of their work make a difference. As a result of this desire to have meaning in the work, early adopters are often impatient with the status quo. If the work is not meaningful and impactful, it is not satisfying. For the dancer in the organization, when the work does not seem significant in one organization the dancer will quickly look to move to another organization.

The great news, however, is that these "dancers" exist in every school and in every school district. They have a winning and willing attitude that is demonstrated over time. They are waiting to dance…to make a difference (M. Moyer, personal communication, May 11, 2016).

For too many leaders, recognizing the potential these early adopters have on the ability of the organization to reach its goals does not occur.

Early adopters by their nature are not passive. These dancers do not feel the need to wait for a consensus from colleagues before trying new approaches to reach their goals. It is a leadership mistake to ask them to wait for consensus from all stakeholders before trying innovative approaches to teaching and learning.

Often, by the time consensus is reached, if at all, months and years of opportunity have passed. By then, while the leadership team was working to build unanimity, or at least a strong consensus to take action, the early adopters will have become frustrated or left the organization altogether for a leadership team or a school culture that values innovation and risk taking in pursuit of the primary mission.

It is not uncommon for schools and school districts to get reputations as organizations that either foster innovation, creativity, and risk taking or as institutions that are hesitant, reluctant, or simply hostile to change. All schools and districts have reputations, brands that address multiple aspects of the organization's perceived culture, whether it is a reputation regarding school safety, student academic performance, or in this case, teacher empowerment.

School and district leaders are no different. Each leader is perceived in various ways by all stakeholders. Each leader has a reputation that precedes the leader. Where the overall reputation of the leader is positive and employees are satisfied with the performance of the leader, employee satisfaction rises and remains high. Where employees are dissatisfied with the effectiveness of the leader, employee satisfaction drops and remains low.

How leaders are perceived regarding the value they place on supporting early adopters and stakeholders willing to take educated risks to advance worthy causes and how leaders react to the organization's dancers will go a long way in determining which of these two reputations is earned and recognized.

It is critical for leaders to understand that most innovation and meaningful change is not the result of consensus from a large group of stakeholders but is the result of a few determined, mission-driven individuals willing to risk the uncertainty of change in order to grow. In fact, most innovation begins with one innovator or a small team of innovators (Kanter, 2000). Simply put, where the innovators are stifled by the organization, there will be no innovation.

These dancers may or may not succeed with the innovations they undertake, but they will learn from their efforts and so will the leaders who support their efforts. There is as much to learn from failure as there is from success. When those early efforts succeed, however, the majority of the organization will join in.

The support needed for the innovation to become a common practice within the organization is the result of the early success, the trial and error, that early adopters undertake. It is the early success of the early adopters that provides more colleagues with the confidence to join the effort, until finally a consensus is reached that the practice in question is effective and worth pursuing on a large scale.

A leadership commitment to dance with the dancers does not occur by accident. Leaders and leadership teams need to support culture-building practices that recognize and reward innovation and continuous improvement (growth) mind-sets. Leaders need to provide the resources, both the financial support and the time needed, for early adopters to plan, test, and implement pilot projects. The efforts of the organization's dancers must be recognized and celebrated (Crosbie, 2005).

Most importantly, leaders need to give the organization's dancers permission to fail. This support by the leader to empower the early adopter, like the Tier 3 leadership strategies discussed in earlier chapters, must become part of the daily routine, the daily habits, of the leader.

FIND THE DANCERS AND START DANCING

There is an overwhelming consensus in the literature regarding leadership in the twenty-first century and building teams, recognizing and empowering talent within the organization, and facilitating the work of others. The fundamental truth of twenty-first-century leadership is that leaders cannot lead alone. Leaders cannot rely on position power, or even expert power, to achieve the organization's goals.

Leaders must recognize the need to build and empower teams of leaders. Knowing that leaders cannot lead effectively alone, in a vacuum, high-impact leaders focus, as a major priority, on identifying, teaming with, and empowering others who share the organization's core mission and values. These early adopters, these dancers, are critical to the leader's success in mission and team building. The good news is that finding these early adopters, these leaders, is not hard. By their very nature, early adopters are ambitious and proactive. They are visible to the leader if the leader will just look. These colleagues are waiting for opportunities to make a difference.

Why, then, are so many dancers, in so many schools, not explicitly involved with the leadership team? For many leaders, the answer is simple: The leader is not looking to expand the leadership team or to introduce innovation into the organization.

These leaders have a management mind-set. These leaders do not see themselves as change agents. These leaders are often overwhelmed with managing the organization rather than growing the capacity of the organization to manage itself. These leaders may be conservative in their approach to change and innovation. These leaders may see innovation as always flowing from the top of the organizational structure down to the school level. The leader who is disconnected from the organization's dancers is literally waiting for superiors to announce innovation and then plan ways to implement that innovation.

DON'T BE AFRAID

Another reason leaders may ignore or resist the organization's dancers is fear. Often, leaders are threatened by these early adopters. A fear of becoming overshadowed or of losing control of the organization may be a concern. Other leaders may feel that it is a primary function of leadership to always be in charge. Delegating meaningful power to others may be seen as a sign of weakness or lack of expertise. Fear of losing control becomes an obstacle to truly bringing these ambitious colleagues onto the leadership team.

This leadership attitude of placing, as the highest priority, the ability to always be in power, to always be the decision-maker, to always be in the room where leadership planning and decision-making is occurring, is a critical mistake and one that high-impact leaders must avoid on a daily basis. Leaders should not fear empowering early adopters; they should fear not empowering early adopters. High-performing organizations are organizations in which groups are empowered to take risks and innovate (Fry, 2003).

THE STATUS QUO IS NOT A FRIEND

Leaders avoiding the dance of innovation may also simply feel that no change or innovation is needed. These leaders may believe that the system is bombarded by what seems like constant change. Every year there are new regulations and policies. Every year there are new best practices and procedures to implement. These leaders may simply wish to protect their colleagues from becoming "burned out" on the pace of change itself.

While there can be no argument that schools and school systems are bombarded by change and an inherent lack of stability, what separates this type of change from the change brought by early adopters is the locus of control for that change. The change that is feared by leaders described above is change that comes from outside the organization with little or no input or local control. The change that dancers bring is internally generated and under the control of those seeking the change.

Perhaps these leaders see the school or school district as running like a finely tuned machine. Perhaps the school has a high state rating. Perhaps strong graduation or promotion rates are evident. For this leader, innovating dancers aren't a threat; they are just unnecessary. The danger in this view is that excellence achieved cannot be excellence sustained without thoughtful but constant innovation. Once leaders and stakeholders believe there is nothing more to accomplish, the possibility to accomplish more is gone.

For leaders who are recognizing that innovation is always worth trying and that the status quo can never be good enough, truly partnering with the early adopters in the organization is necessary. After all, these dancers share the leader's mission and goals. These dancers want to support the leader. Effective and impactful leadership in education is a team sport. Highly effective leaders begin by building that team with the organization's dancers as the first members of the team.

POWER TO THE DANCERS

High-impact Tier 3 leaders empower the "first followers" in the system with leadership time, expertise, and support. There is a recognition that these early adopters will impact the effectiveness of the leader and the organization in significant ways (Riggio, Chaleff, & Lipman-Bluman, 2008). These leaders also recognize that there is a significant difference between giving stakeholders the authority or permission to innovate and giving stakeholders the support and tools they need to actually innovate. For dancers to succeed, the leader must be much more than words or attitude; the leader must be action oriented.

When a leader says they are more than willing to have new ideas and approaches "bubble up" from members of the organization, but at the same time provides no formal support structure for those stakeholders to innovate, the leader is not investing in the dancers. Lip service is not power.

A dancer needs a dance floor, a place to dance. A dancer needs the time to dance. A dancer needs the opportunity to practice, to evaluate, and to team up with other dancers. Leaders can provide all of these resources and demonstrate by their actions that support for the early adopter. If the infrastructure of time, money, and intellectual support is not in place, the leader is not empowering the innovators in the organization. Permission is not enough. The capacity to implement must also be there. It is the leader's responsibility to provide that capacity.

DISTRIBUTE AUTHORITY, NOT TASKS

True innovation is, by its nature, organic. Innovation is not an assignment or a task to be accomplished. Innovation is not something that can be delegated. Too often, leaders believe that they are distributing leadership when, in fact, the leader is simply distributing assignments. Completing to-do lists are not how early adopters innovate.

Delegation is an effective management leadership trait, and there are certainly proper ways to delegate and poor ways to delegate, but delegation is not the proper tool for building cultures that innovate. In fact, the more constraints a leader places on the dancers within the organization, the less likely those dancers are to truly innovate or to be truly motivated toward the work.

Innovation can, however, be encouraged and supported by specific leadership behaviors. Innovation is most likely to occur when the authority to try new approaches is valued by the culture and encouraged, in word, and in deed, by the leadership team. The organization's dancers must know that innovation and risk on behalf of the overall mission of the organization is encouraged and that failure is not something to fear, but an expected by-product of the innovative process.

In addition, how the leader reacts to failure is critical. Tier 3 leaders see failure as a learning opportunity. For many leaders, however, failure is seen as the one thing that must be avoided at all costs. Dancers cannot dance, innovators cannot innovate, in cultures that fear failure.

Let your early adopters plan their next steps. The sharing of responsibility with a team of expert stakeholders who are committed to the mission should also include the authority to plan, and most importantly, to revise action plans and implementation strategies as the team proceeds. If every change in strategy needs to be signed off on by the leader, micromanaging is sure to follow. Leaders who micromanage are viewed by colleagues as intrusive at best and demonstrating a lack of trust and confidence in the team at worst. Early adopters in particular will chafe at leadership behavior that micromanages their work.

This does not mean that the team has the authority to change the process systems that are in place to ensure transparency and consistency that have been established as organizational norms. This certainly does not mean that the authority to change the overall mission or primary goals and objectives of the organization have been delegated. Mission and process goals should involve the widest possible spectrum of internal and external stakeholders in their development and in their revisions. It is these processes that build the culture and climate to support the innovations of the dancers in the first place.

For all other delegated activity to the team, however, Tier 3 leaders distribute the authority to review and revise implementation plans as warranted. These leaders then use the systems that have been built for ensuring timely and thorough communication between leaders and leadership teams to both stay "in the loop" and to provide expert advice as needed.

TURN OFF THE CLOCK

Tier 3 leaders have the team assume the responsibility to manage and monitor their processes and their progress. Just as innovation cannot be delegated, it also cannot be timed. Creativity tied to a stopwatch is not a recipe for innovation or success. This is not to say that leaders do not need to communicate on a regular basis with the organization's early adopters.

It is important for the dancers in the system to have their voices heard, and to hear the mission voice of the leader. It is important for the leadership team to know what support the dancers need or what obstacles to innovation the dancers are facing. When the leadership team is seeking information from the dancers, the first priority should not be to find out what has been accomplished; the first priority should be to find out what support the dancers need to continue their work. Specific time limits or due dates for deliverables are counter to the efforts of both the early adopters and the leaders wishing to support the work.

SUCCESS IS?

All organizations have goals and measurable program outcomes. The public education sector in particular is highly accountable to a wide, and increasing, range of student learning outcomes as well as teacher performance outcomes. Every leader must measure progress toward those system goals and be accountable for leading teams toward accomplishing those targets. Working with the early adopters of the organization and establishing goals for those early adopters to reach is counterproductive, however.

The definition of success for early adopters is innovation and creating new and different ways to accomplish the mission of the organization. For these dancers, having external definitions of success will not prove to be productive any more than having external time constraints for delivering the innovation itself. Tier 3 leaders allow the team to develop their own criteria for success, their own targets to achieve, and their own systems to evaluate their outcomes. The Tier 3 leader trusts the dancers to dance in ways that have the potential to bring the organization closer to its primary mission.

CELEBRATE, CELEBRATE, DANCE TO THE MUSIC

Tier 3 leaders find multiple ways to celebrate the dancers in the organization. Tier 3 leaders prioritize celebrating successes big and small as critical to the overall climate of the organization. It has been said that to understand what a culture values, look at what the culture celebrates.

Celebrating a culture of innovation must be an organic part of the organization's behavior. Single events, like award ceremonies, or faculty highlights in the end-of-year newsletter, may be one way to recognize accomplishments of stakeholders, but they are not, in and of themselves, culture-building or climate-sustaining activities. Highlighting the accomplishments of innovators once a year does not build a culture of innovation any more than the end-of-the-year award assembly for students with perfect attendance builds a culture that values learning.

The recognition from the leadership team to all of the organization's stakeholders that a culture of innovation, of risk taking, is valued is an important component for success. Celebrations that occur throughout the culture should emphasize the effort, the process, that innovators take, not the outcome. It is one thing to celebrate innovation that has worked and made a profound impact on the organization. It is another, and perhaps more valuable, thing to celebrate the efforts of early adopters whose work may not have resulted in the intended outcomes of those involved.

As mentioned earlier, changing the paradigm that failure is the worst thing that can happen to a school, a team, or an individual is a critical component of innovative organizational cultures. These cultures recognize that failure is often a prerequisite for meaningful success; that it is what we learn from our failures that matters.

TODAY IS A GOOD DAY TO DANCE WITH THE DANCERS

1. Today is a good day to work with early adopters who are mission driven, and empower them with leadership support.
2. Today is a good day to ask the dancers what they would do if they could do anything to achieve the mission. Early adopters are, by their nature, creative risk takers who see opportunities where others see obstacles. By asking these early adopters to think creatively and boldly, leaders are very likely to receive a broad array of new ideas and possibilities that can impact the mission in a positive way.
3. Today is a good day to celebrate the efforts of the early adopters in the organization. When bad news occurs, everyone in the organization is certain to be aware. Can the same be said for the good news? For high-impact leaders, the answer to that question is yes. What is valued in the culture gets celebrated. If nothing is being celebrated, then nothing is truly valued.
4. Today is a good day to identify stakeholders who are waiting to be invited to the leadership dance. Not every dancer, every early adopter, or every first follower is an extrovert. Every system has high-performing dancers who are simply waiting to be asked to participate, to lead. Tier 3 leaders find those dancers and invite them to the dance.
5. Today is a good day to celebrate the efforts of innovators whose work did not achieve the intended outcome but did demonstrate a culture of continuous improvement. How a culture reacts to failure will say as much about the overall climate of the organization as looking at how a culture reacts to success. Tier 3 leaders see failure as a learning opportunity. Tier 3 leaders encourage innovation and risk taking and accept that not every initiative will succeed.
6. Today is a good day to assess whether or not there is significant leadership activity designed to empower others. High-performing leaders don't just monitor results or processes; they are also monitoring the degree to which significant missions/tasks have been distributed throughout the organization.

Chapter Thirteen

Dance with the Silent

Impactful leaders recognize that all high-performing schools or school districts are made up of teams. No one person has the time or the expertise to lead organizations as complex as schools and school districts on their own. Even if the leader was attempting to lead in isolation, informal teams and leaders would emerge within, and impact the organization (Mehra, Smith, Dixon, & Robertson, 2006).

Teams will always emerge, and teams will always influence the organization. High-performing leaders recognize that it is the power of the team on a common mission that matters most. Leaders wishing to influence teams recognize that for teams to be effective, they must not only be mission driven, but they also must be diverse and powerful. These teams must represent all of the members of the organization, both internal and external. These teams must not be micromanaged by leadership, but be granted the authority to make leadership decisions that will impact the organization in significant ways (Amabile, Schatzel, Moneta, & Kramer, 2003).

In effective teams, every member has a role to play and feels connected to the team's mission. Too often, even those leaders who are committed to the power of the team, and who recognize that effective leadership is team leadership, fail to recognize that impactful teams are made up of more than mission-driven employees within the organization, but also include those reluctant employees and stakeholders outside the organization. In effective schools, these teams are made up of diverse members of the school organization along with external stakeholders, including those silent members of the organization.

Chapter 12 discussed the many powerful ways that the organization's early adopters, the dancers, can have a profound impact on the success of the organization. In this chapter the roles that the silent or the disenfranchised play on the overall health of the organization are examined.

It is a common mistake for leaders to populate their leadership teams with clones, that is, with members of the organization who think, look, and behave in similar ways as the leader. These teams will never be able to capitalize on the experiences and expertise of a diverse group of individuals.

Teams that lack diversity, in every sense of the word, are by their very nature diminished (Rowe, 2003). Cloned teams are typically populated only with the early adopters, the dancers, only with the members of the organization who are proactive and who will quickly adopt the mission and vision of the organization's leader. It is true that these early followers are critical to the success of the organization and the vitality of the team. They are necessary for success. They are not, however, sufficient for success.

High-performing leaders must also connect with the silent members of the organization. These silent employees and stakeholders tend to fall into two categories. First, there are the silent external stakeholders who don't know how the organization works and communicates or who don't feel welcome within the organization. These individuals are silent out of a sense of disconnectedness or a feeling that they don't have the expertise to offer anything of value to the organization.

Many parents fall into this category. These parents feel intimidated by the school, by the complex language used by school leaders, and by a sense that the system is too big for their voices to be truly heard. These silent members may also feel that their voices are not welcomed or valued by those in charge. Often these individuals are limited in their position power.

Internal members of the organization can also be silent. Support staff, beginning teachers, and students who are not comfortable with the language and processes associated with school environments are all examples of stakeholders who tend to be part of the silent class. These are the stakeholders who interact with the school but who do not speak and who are not heard. Too many school cultures diminish the voices of these individuals in subtle and overt ways. Beginning teachers are told to stay quiet and pay their dues. Support staff are seen but not heard. Students receive all of the system rules and expectations, but have no voice in creating the system rules or expectations.

Some of these silent members of the organization are simply waiting for an invitation to participate. In these schools, just being invited to participate will spur the colleague or stakeholder on to meaningful participation. If not invited and actively sought out, these individuals will remain unheard. If sought out and valued for their expertise and experiences, these same individuals will easily and actively engage.

A second category of silent stakeholders are those individuals who have strong opinions but are hostile to the mission of the organization and have purposely disconnected from the work of the organization. These individuals have lost any belief that what they have to say will ever be heard or acted upon by leadership. These stakeholders believe the system is rigged, and because their voices would never be taken seriously anyway, why even engage? These individuals will be more reluctant than the first category of silent stakeholders to take on any role within the organization and are particularly reluctant to take on a visible role.

Some of these individuals may also believe that it is easier and more comfortable to criticize the leaders and the systems put in place if they are not engaged in the process at all. For these individuals it is easier to remain on the sidelines as a silent critic, or remain on the sidelines as a vocal antagonist, rather than get involved in trying to change the organization's goals or culture by working within the confines of the organization's teams and structures.

The high-performing leader recognizes that both of these groups of silent stakeholders still have a valuable role to play; they have potential to contribute beyond their current performance. The high-impact Tier 3 leader recognizes that it is the job of the leader to reach out to the silent, not to expect the silent to somehow reach out to the leader or leadership teams.

Finally, the Tier 3 leader recognizes that this work, the work of reaching out to the silent, requires daily attention. Intermittent attention to who the silent stakeholders are or learning how to engage with these silent stakeholders does not work. Strategies to engage with, to dance with, the silent must be thought about and implemented each and every day. Fortunately there are many strategies that Tier 3 leaders can use to bring the silent and the reluctant stakeholder to the leadership table.

BE THERE

High-impact Tier 3 leaders commit to meeting with reluctant colleagues on their turf and on their time. Too often, leaders work primarily out of their offices, their conference rooms, or other administrative offices. It is not uncommon for leaders to spend 50 percent, 60 percent, or 70 percent of the day or longer busy but confined in the main administrative office or related work spaces. Since meetings are scheduled through the office manager and are typically held in administrative offices or conference rooms, leaders often spend most of the workday in these locations. This type of scheduling can certainly increase efficiency, but it has the negative side effect of isolating the leader within the administrative quarters.

While active members of the organization will make their way to the leader's offices, those reluctant members of the school community certainly will not. What good is having an open-door policy if large segments of stakeholders never walk through that door? In addition, requiring all stakeholders to come to the leader's office can also create an intimidating setting for those members of the organization or community who are not comfortable with school organizations and hierarchies in the first place. Particularly for the silent, non-involved stakeholder, the strategy of meeting with those individuals on the leader's turf can be counterproductive.

Instead, effective Tier 3 leaders make a significant effort to meet with these reluctant (silent) colleagues on their turf. Tier 3 leaders dance with the silent where the silent live, not where the leader lives. They are willing to go outside of the normal locations and offices of power out into the school to meet with silent internal stakeholders and out into the community to meet with silent external stakeholders.

WHOSE SCHEDULE IS IT?

In addition to being willing to meet outside of the leader' office, it is important for the leader to also engage silent colleagues at times that work best for them, not necessarily for the leader. Too often, meetings are scheduled around the leader's calendar. What time of day works best for the leader? When is the leader available? If those times are not what work best for colleagues, then it is expected that the colleagues will need to adjust their schedules.

Perhaps the teacher needs to give up their planning period in order to meet. Perhaps the leader sends a substitute teacher or teacher aide down to the teacher's classroom to cover the class for thirty minutes so the teacher can meet with the principal at a time that works best for the principal. Perhaps the parent conference is scheduled when it is best for the teacher or leader to meet with the parent regardless of the disruption to the parent's day.

While all of these strategies and reasons for using them are sound, a subtle message is also being sent. That message is this: The leader's time is more valuable than the follower's time; the leader's time is more valuable than the parent's time. The leader may want to engage with the silent or reluctant stakeholder, but only on the leader's terms.

A far different message is sent when the leader begins to reach out to silent or reluctant colleagues by asking, "What is a good time and location for you to meet with me? I am flexible and want to meet with you at a time that works best for your schedule. You are doing me a favor by taking the time to talk with me, and I want to honor that time that you are providing." There are already enough challenges involved in achieving meaningful communication and engagement with reluctant colleagues. Forcing reluctant colleagues to meet at a time and location that serves the convenience of the leader at the expense of the colleague is counterproductive.

IT IS ALL THE STUDENTS

Tier 3 leaders make it a habit to meet with diverse groups of students each day. Just as leaders are prone to interact with teachers and other staff who are supportive of the leader and the leader's goals, it is also common for leaders to want to interact primarily with students who are supportive of the school and the direction that the leadership team is taking.

There are many formal organizations in place made up of these types of student supporters. The school student government association, the band, athletic clubs, and class clubs are all examples of systems in place that are accepting of engaged student behavior and are easy for engaged students to join, have a voice, and easily interact with the leader. When schools support and expand the opportunities for students to serve as real leaders, not only does the student benefit from learning and practicing important life skills, the entire organization and leadership team also benefit (Cahill, 2006).

These are the organizations that are filled with the student dancers within the school. Like the faculty and other adult dancers associated with the school, it is critical that the leader and the leadership teams remain actively engaged with these student dancers. It is a necessary component of the success of any school enterprise to engage with these students in meaningful ways (Leithwood & Jantzi, 2008).

As with the silent adult stakeholders, however, engaging with the student dancers only is not sufficient to maximize the success of the school goals and build a truly positive and engaging climate. Tier 3 leaders also recognize the importance of reaching out to, and engaging with, the silent or disengaged student.

In order to reach out to these students, the leader needs to know who these students are and where they are. This group of students cannot be found in the school clubs, they are typically not found in the dean's office, they are often not on the list of at-risk students or the list of honor roll or perfect attendance students; these are the students living in the undefined middle of the school culture. These are the students who are at school but not engaged with school.

It should be a daily objective for every school leader to identify and interact with at least one, if not more, of these silent students each day. These interactions do not need to be long, but they do need to be meaningful. A brief conversation in the hallway, the opportunity to have breakfast or lunch with a group of silent students, a brief phone call or text message that is supportive of these students—all of these are examples of leadership activity that does not take a great deal of time, but over time results in meaningful engagement with a large, often-unrecognized sector of the school student population: the silent, disengaged student.

IT IS THE ADULTS IN THE BUILDING

Because not every member of the organization is an early adopter, it is a near-certainty that the many silent members of the organization, both by their own choice and by the choices made by leaders, will not be participants in the organizational structures that make the entire system work. High-impact leaders think about who these non-participating colleagues and external stakeholders are. Where do they work in the organization? How are they assigned throughout the organization? Are there certain departments or grade levels that tend to have a significant number of non-participants within that particular sector of the organization?

Questions like this need to be asked and the answers need to be clearly understood by the leader and everyone involved in expanding the makeup and diversity of the leadership team. Leaders cannot implement purposeful strategies to dance with the silent if they don't understand who the silent really are.

Once leaders have a clear understanding of who the non-participants are, and where they reside, leaders should reach out to these colleagues in a variety of ways to try to foster real engagement. The goal of the leader is to work on a daily basis to open new lines of communication with these silent members of the team and to find ways to bring them into the decision-making processes and the implementation work that is taking place to meet the organization's goals.

Not every member of this silent sector will be open, even after the best of intentions and efforts by the leader, to serving as a member of a leadership team. For some of these individuals, success may consist of opening meaningful communication between members of leadership and the individual in ways that are informal and not part of committee work- or task-force activity. It is a sign of success when real dialogue and communication occurs with colleagues who before did not engage, even if those new lines of communication are private or, at first, limited.

For other members of the organization, however, just being asked to join in leadership activity and decision-making opportunities will spur those individuals into action. In every organization there are the silent members who are simply waiting to be asked to join the dance. Tier 3 leaders ask.

IT'S THE ADULTS OUTSIDE THE BUILDING

Tier 3 leaders also recognize that the vast majority of adults in the community are not connected with the school or school system in any meaningful way. These leaders will identify those adults that are not represented in the organization's leadership and operation systems.

One simple strategy is not to let a day go by without some form of parent and/or student communication. If the leader is reaching out on a daily basis to parents, business leaders, and other engaged citizens about what is happening in their hometown schools, word of that school progress will begin to spread. If every member of the leadership team is doing the same thing on a daily basis, the impact of that outreach will grow exponentially.

Today's schools have more internal and external stakeholders than ever before. The external stakeholders vested in the performance and success of the school, and the school district, can include policymakers at the national, state, and local levels; business leaders; senior citizens; real estate agents; school board members—the list goes on and on. It can be an easy leadership trap to become overwhelmed with attempting to meet the needs of such a large number of constituents.

It is also an easy, but dangerous response to the complexity of the work, and the need to stay focused on what is happening within the school, for leaders to delegate most, or all, of their outreach efforts to subordinates. The department chair is assigned to run PTA meetings. The athletic director is assigned to run athletic booster meetings. The junior member of the administrative team is assigned to sit in on any potentially contentious parent-teacher conferences.

While all of these leadership strategies may be necessary due to the amount of communication occurring with internal and external stakeholders, Tier 3 leaders know that their daily schedules should include some type of outreach and communication with these same constituencies.

No group of stakeholders, however, is more important than the students served by the school and the parents who entrust their children to the school and the educators therein. Impact leaders make it a top priority to reach out to students and parents each day. Impact leaders do not delegate this task to others, but recognize that as the individual in the highest position of power and authority, they must model continuous communication and outreach.

At the same time, leaders who are committed to ongoing communication with all parents and students, particularly those parents and students who are not active in the school, recognize that dancing with these silent stakeholders takes the concerted and organized efforts of the entire leadership team. Not only should the leader reach out to some individual parent or student, or some small group of parents and students, on a daily basis, so should every member of the leadership team.

FACEBOOK AND TWITTER, TO NAME A FEW

Tier 3 leaders recognize that communication comes in many forms. These high-performing leaders tend to embrace and expand their use of social media to reach as many constituencies as possible (Sweetser & Kelleher, 2011). How schools are perceived; how leaders are judged; how the climate and culture of each classroom, the school, and the district are interpreted by internal and external stakeholders—all of these are subject to an instant and ubiquitous onslaught of social media.

In this environment, leaders have two fundamental choices: Choice one, do not engage with social media and continue to use traditional forms of communication as the only or primary source of reaching out to stakeholders, particularly those external stakeholders who only understand or interact with the school or district from a distance. Choice two, engage with social media, using it as a valuable tool to share the organization's goals, culture, and accomplishments, big and small.

Every school and school district leader—in fact, every classroom teacher—is under discussion and evaluation by internal and external stakeholders on a daily basis, via Twitter, Facebook, and all of the other forms of social media in use today. Opinions and judgments are being formed about the leader and the organization, whether or not the leader is engaged in the conversation (Schafer & Taddicken, 2015). The question is not whether social media is being used to shape the perceptions of the school or the school district by multiple groups, within and without the school system; the question is whether the leadership team is engaged in the process, as well.

High-impact Tier 3 leaders do not let a day go by without communicating via social media. That communication does not need to be limited only to significant activity or accomplishments or information needed about the day. It can be as simple as congratulating an individual student or teacher for a job well done. It can be a thank-you to a local business for their support of the school. The important aspect of this type of communication activity is that it occurs on a daily basis, without fail.

PLAN IT OUT

Effective leaders build formal structures to involve external stakeholders in the work of the school or district. Bridging the gap between the classroom, the school, or the district and disengaged stakeholders cannot be accomplished without goal setting, strategic planning, and ongoing progress monitoring. While random efforts to increase outreach may make a small difference, it is only when formal structures are put into place that meaningful success and impact will occur.

These formal structures should include goals, timelines, and the designation of team members who will be responsible for program implementation, measurable outcomes, and progress monitoring by the entire leadership structure of the organization. Building these formal structures and then monitoring their implementation and success should be part of the daily routine. As with internal stakeholders, this planning should include building systems that ensure that meetings occur with external stakeholders on their turf and on their time.

Leaders and their team members who are committed to building bridges between the school and the community recognize that bridge building is a two-way street. Often, leaders build bridges—outreach plans to the larger external community—but those bridges function like a one-way street, in which the expectation is for the stakeholders to come to the school, not for the school to go to the stakeholders.

Too often, school leaders build these communication opportunities around a schedule that is most convenient for school employees but not convenient for parents or other external stakeholders. If meetings are being scheduled in the afternoon, when many constituents are working, true outreach is not occurring. If weekdays are when all meeting opportunities are being held but weekends are when many stakeholders have the time to meet, true outreach is not occurring.

Impact leaders change this dynamic by developing and implementing a robust communication plan that takes school leaders out into the community to both share the mission and vision of the school and to learn firsthand from constituents those areas of pride and concern that may be occurring regarding the school.

While no leader or leadership team will be able to successfully integrate all stakeholders, those who are connected to the organization, into meaningful active roles within the organization, when leaders work on a daily basis to "dance with the silent," more voices and expertise will come forward. There are many more silent stakeholders than there are active stakeholders. Connecting with these constituents is a critical component for building transparency, communication, and a sense of community and common mission between schools, school districts, and the communities they serve.

These connections do not happen without a committed effort by the entire leadership structure of the organization. These connections do not happen unless the culture and the climate of the school recognize the importance of the outreach. How leaders engage with all stakeholders, and the degree to which leaders commit to bringing all stakeholders impacted by the decisions being made into the decision-making process, will have an impact on stakeholder resistance (Lundy & Morin, 2013).

As more voices are sought out and heard, an interest in, and a willingness to, become involved in the success of the school will be more easily established, and a true sense of team and common purpose is more likely to become the cultural norm of the organization. If the smartest person in the room is the room, it makes sense that the larger the room, the smarter the room. Impact leaders increase the size of the room by dancing with the silent on a daily basis.

TODAY IS A GOOD DAY TO DANCE WITH THE SILENT

1. Today is a good day to add someone new to a leadership team. In every organization, there are large numbers of colleagues who can contribute to the mission if asked. High-performing leaders ask.
2. Today is a good day to reach out the unsung heroes of your organization, whoever they are, and let them know how much they matter. Tier 3 leaders take a few minutes each and every day to send a note, make a phone call, or speak directly to a colleague who is making a difference. Often these unsung contributors are working in positions without power or prestige. Effective leaders find these colleagues and thank them for all they do.
3. Today is a good day to contact a parent who has not heard good news from the school in the past. For far too many parents, the only time they hear from the school is when there is some type of problem. A call from the school is always bad news. Each day, however, the vast majority of students are working hard and doing exactly what is being asked of them by the adults in the school. The leader, and all of the adults in the building, should be reaching out to these parents, and to the students themselves, to say thank you for a job well done. This outreach does not take much time if done on a regular basis by everyone in the system.
4. Today is a good day to reach out to a student who is silent but successful and let them know you see their effort. For most schools, the highest-performing students and the lowest-performing students are being interacted with on a regular basis by the educators in the building. But there is a silent majority of students who are neither high performing, nor low performing but are working hard to make something of themselves and their school experience. Tier 3 leaders reach out and establish ongoing lines of communication with these students.
5. Today is a good day to expand your communication outreach through social media. While traditional forms of communication and outreach, like the school newsletter, the open house, and the monthly school PTA meeting, can certainly be effective, they are by no means adequate. Effective leaders recognize that powerful and ongoing communication is critical to getting the good news out to the community, as well as in contextualizing and adding needed information regarding any issues the school may be dealing with.

6. Today is a good day to empower those without position power with meaningful work. Impact leaders don't just delegate work to others; they empower others to complete meaningful tasks by giving those colleagues the authority and the resources necessary to do the work.
7. Today is a good day to identify one parent, one student, and one teacher who have not yet been asked for their input—and ask. Schools and school systems with motivated and engaged parents, students, and teachers are always going to outperform schools and school systems with disengaged and unmotivated parents, students, and teachers. Engagement does not occur by accident; it is the result of a series of ongoing outreach behaviors by the leadership team.

Chapter Fourteen

Avoid Isolation and Embrace Inquiry

Isolation is the enemy of effective leadership. As discussed throughout this book, leadership in the twenty-first century is a team sport. The notion of a single leader as sufficient to bring an entire organizational culture and climate to its full potential is not only an antiquated concept, but it is an organizational structure doomed to failure. High-impact leaders develop others, and high-impact leaders distribute authority and the capacity to lead and shape the direction of the organization over to teams of leaders (Harris & Lambert, 2003).

High-impact leaders recognize a fundamental truth about educational leadership: No one individual can do it alone. The tenth, and perhaps most important daily behavior for high-impact leadership involves strategies to avoid isolation in all of its forms. Isolation can manifest itself in multiple ways: physical isolation, intellectual isolation, and mission isolation (Colwell, 2015). Taking deliberate steps to avoid isolation in all of its forms each day is necessary for impactful leadership.

PHYSICAL ISOLATION

The office is a dangerous place for leaders to be, and yet it is where many leaders spend the vast majority of their time. True, the office is where meetings can easily occur. It is the official headquarters of the leader. Leaders will often rationalize the amount of time spent working from the office, because it seems faster and more efficient to have stakeholders come to the leader's office than to have the leader moving from place to place.

The office is where most of the technology for communicating resides. Everyone knows where the leader's office is, so everyone will always know where to find the leader. Leaders who are office bound will tell others that it seems easier to deal with e-mails, make phone calls, coordinate the activities of staff members, and centralize operations from the office.

Add in all of the unscheduled events that occur, and it is easy to see how the leader can become office bound. Even though today's mobile technology should reduce the leader's reliance on being office bound, the tendency to see the office as "leadership headquarters" is strong. Why, then, is the office a dangerous place for the twenty-first-century school leader?

While there are clearly efficiencies in being able to coordinate activities from one central office, those activities are often limited to management or reactive problem-solving. Tier 3 activities taking place in the leader's office, interpersonal skill-building activities, are probably occurring only on a limited scale. Unless the leader has complete control of the calendar and how meetings will be scheduled, under what circumstances meetings will be added to the agenda or cancelled, the office can quickly deteriorate into a place where firefighting and daily management activities occur, to the exclusion of Tier 2 and Tier 3 leadership activities.

The office can be a great place to hold a confidential meeting with one or two colleagues. It is not, however, a great place from which to lead teams or build the capacity of the overall organization. It is critical for every leader to remember that the mission of the school is not occurring in the administrator's office; it is occurring where the teachers and students are. It is occurring where the stakeholders are. Leaders can't build relationships from behind a desk or over the phone. Leaders can't articulate a mission that they never, or rarely see in action.

Instructional leadership occurs where instruction is occurring. Interpersonal team-building leadership activity occurs where the stakeholder teams are working. Leaders develop by enhancing the quality of their professional relationships with peers and with subordinates by serving as a coach and mentor to others out in the field, and by being coached by others (Robertson, 2016). This requires that the high-performing leader be visible, to be where the students and other stakeholders are. Their goal is not to have an "open door" policy, but rather a "no door" practice. Tier 3 leaders get out of the office.

INTELLECTUAL ISOLATION

Take a moment to think about the people you know whom you perceive to be smart. Everyone knows someone who seems able to solve complex problems or explain complex issues in terms that are clear to everyone. These individuals are often seen as more than just experts on any particular subject. They are seen as intellectually gifted in the largest sense of the word. These individuals appear to have the ability to think clearly and creatively, to understand things that most people don't understand.

While there are fields of study that require a great deal of technical expertise, the ability to master complex fields of inquiry is not the sole determiner of intelligence. Individuals who are recognized by their peers as intellectuals may not be smarter than everyone else. They may, however, be employing a specific set of behaviors and attitudes that are then viewed by peers and stakeholders as signs of intelligence.

GET INTERESTED

It is the power of inquiry that helps separate out the individuals who are seen as smart from everyone else. One of the things that "smart" people do differently is not to understand more than almost everyone else, but to ask more questions than almost everyone else. Human beings are inquisitive by nature. When we look at children we perceive to be smart, what we see are children asking questions, always wanting to learn things. What is a common refrain from the toddler? "Why, why, why?"

Sadly, for most people, that sense of interest and inquiry fades over time. For those who are perceived by others as having brain power, that genuine interest in the nature of the world remains intact past childhood. Smart people are not necessarily smarter than everyone else; they are just more curious than everyone else. These people don't know more answers; they ask more questions and understand the amazing power of inquiry.

Intellectual isolation is the failure to inquire, the failure to be genuinely interested in how things work, the failure to be interested in what other people think, the failure to consider the possibilities of what could be. The good news is that inquiry-based behaviors can be practiced and learned. Intellectual isolation is a choice. Just as most people can, with practice, acquire new skills, such as learning a new language or how to play a musical instrument, leaders can also learn to question more, to be interested.

The power of inquiry is one of the building blocks for the ability to think creatively. The power of inquiry is a prerequisite for effective collaboration and innovation (Jamison, Ferrell, Kelly, et al., 2006). Not only do leaders need to be intellectually engaged in their work and with their colleagues, but high-impact leaders need to surround themselves with other inquirers. High-performing teams are teams asking questions; they want to learn. Intellectual isolation poses a very real threat to leadership effectiveness. Tier 3 leaders want to learn something new each day by asking questions.

MISSION ISOLATION

Earlier in this book, the fundamental question, "Why should anyone be led by you?" was asked. The answer involved the belief in the power of a mission-driven, team-oriented approach to leadership. A leader with no followers is not a leader. Followers need much more than a leader to follow, however; they also need a reason to follow. What motivates people to strive for greatness, to stretch their capacity, to commit to work that is difficult, is the belief that there is a value in the mission.

Stephen Covey describes this belief in working toward something of significance as working for the "big yes" (Covey, 1989). It is the purpose of the work that brings value to the team. Without a purpose, all work becomes routine at best and drudgery at worst. This "big yes" can, in and of itself, be a very charismatic and motivating force in any organization.

Belief is a powerful motivator of human behavior and commitment. Leaders who believe strongly in a powerful mission, and who are able to model that belief in word and deed, are seen as charismatic, not because the leader is a great orator or extrovert, but because the mission that is being articulated has meaning and power.

On the other hand, leaders who don't have a meaningful mission or cannot articulate that mission are in danger of being isolated from the mission of the organization itself, as well as from those followers and stakeholders who do seek a larger purpose in their work. Mission isolation is a common condition for too many leaders. It can occur because the leader becomes overwhelmed with the responsibilities of management. Mission-driven leadership requires strategic planning. Mission-driven leadership requires what Zenger and Folkman describe as communication that is powerful and relentless (Zenger and Folkman, 2002).

STRATEGIES TO AVOID ISOLATION IN ALL ITS FORMS

Tier 3 leaders understand that how the day is prioritized is critical to avoiding isolation in all of its forms: physical, intellectual, or missional. One simple strategy is to move paperwork and management activity to the very end of the day. Time spent on management activity during instructional time or during a time when stakeholders are available is not time well spent.

There will always be occasions when the demands of daily operations invade the time that could be spent on instructional and interpersonal activities. The key is for the leader to be aware that management activities can interfere with more impactful leadership activities, and to build systems into the day that minimize those incursions. Scheduling management activity into the daily calendar during specific blocks of time that don't conflict with Tier 2 and Tier 3 activity is an important first step. Working with the leadership team to be sure that no one member of the team is overburdened with management responsibilities at the expense of leadership activities is also an important and effective strategy.

Leaders committed to avoiding isolation in all of its forms go where the students and teachers are for several hours each day. For these leaders, time spent where stakeholders are is seen as time that is nonnegotiable.

Every leader has meetings and obligations that are nonnegotiable. When the superintendent calls a mandatory meeting, the leader makes adjustments on the calendar so that the meeting can be attended, and any obligations that are in conflict with the new meeting are also handled. Perhaps the leader delegates the activity to another leader. Perhaps the activity can be moved to another time or date. On any given day, however, there are events that simply must have the leader's participation. Parent conferences involving complex student issues, speeches to external stakeholders, teacher meetings involving significant issues around curriculum and instruction—these are all examples of events that leaders, on a routine basis, should make sure they are attending.

Too often leaders will not make the same level of commitment to working with teachers and students on a daily basis for extended periods of time. The leader may schedule class walk-throughs or visits to routine department or grade-level meetings on the calendar and have every intention of participating in those activities, but if the leader feels there are a large number of more urgent events to attend, it is easy to feel that since these activities can occur on any day, the visit can easily be rescheduled for tomorrow or next week. As the days and weeks pass, the leader will become more and more isolated from the students and teachers.

By setting as a high priority, on a daily basis, time out of the office and time with faculty and students, the leader is much likelier to avoid becoming isolated. For Tier 3 leaders, the time spent with students, teachers, and stakeholders outside of the office is the most valuable and productive use of the leader's time.

Tier 3 leaders keep a daily log of what actually is occurring each day and how much time it is taking. It is common for leaders to have remarkably busy days and yet, at the end of the day, not have a clear understanding of where the day went, and what actually was accomplished. The leader knows the day was busy, perhaps overwhelmingly so. The leader knows that important decisions were made, meetings held, and issues resolved.

When asked, however, for a breakdown of how much time was spent on Tier 1 management activity, how much time was spent on Tier 2 technical/ expert activity, and how much time was spent on Tier 3 interpersonal skill and human development activity, the leader cannot accurately answer the question. Often the time that leaders are actually committing to specific objectives are not even correlated with the leader's own perceived value of those objectives (Ammons & Newell, 1989). As a result, there is no positive correlation between leader priorities and leader time management.

By taking a few minutes each day to log how much time was spent on each activity, and clearly describe the nature of that activity, the leader knows how the workday is actually being spent. This takes discipline and a willingness to honestly track behaviors.

The benefit of this type of self-analysis is significant. By understanding current behavior, the leader can establish goals and priorities to change that behavior. When leaders are able to document that 60 percent, 70 percent, or even 80 percent of the time that is being spent on most days is dedicated to management activity and not to Tier 2 and Tier 3 activity, the leader can think strategically about how to change those percentages. Tier 3 leaders become Tier 3 leaders by logging and analyzing their own behaviors.

Tier 3 leaders ask important questions every day. These questions center on school culture, climate, and larger organizational goals more than the status of routine management activity. These leaders are inquiry-based leaders. They work to understand what other members of the organization think and how they feel about the work and the progress, or lack of progress, that is occurring.

Tier 3 leaders learn how to listen to other members of the organization. Impactful leaders don't ask questions to confirm preconceived notions already held, or to confirm consensus of opinions already determined. Impact leaders don't ask questions about methods or goals they have already decided cannot be changed; regardless of any new information or ideas, they ask questions for one primary reason: to build their own capacity as a team member.

Instead of creating "to do" lists, impact leaders have something like a "to learn" list. All successful leaders have systems in place to help manage multiple activities, due dates, and projects all running at the same time. These "to do" lists may have many different forms and systems in place, but they are all designed to help the leader manage simultaneous activities and projects.

Tier 3 leaders, leaders who are committed to avoiding intellectual isolation, also build systems to ensure that learning is occurring each day. High-impact leaders prioritize the need to stay current by remaining a lifelong learner. High-impact leaders recognize that today's expert can easily be out-of-date tomorrow. For these leaders, learning is not an option; it is a necessity.

Leaders who are committed to avoiding isolation keep track of all stakeholder communication. They know the last time when specific teams of teachers, students, parents, and other stakeholders were heard from. These leaders are committed to the goal of not letting a single day go by without some form of direct communication with at least one team of internal stakeholders (teachers and students) and one team of external stakeholders (PTA, Booster Club members, business leaders). This can only occur if the leader is tracking daily behavior, and is committed to ongoing stakeholder communication.

The research regarding what makes some leaders extraordinary and others average, or worse, has grown significantly over the last ten years. Our understanding of the complex set of skills, values, and attributes that comprise high-performing leadership is more profound and actionable today than ever before. Leaders who are successful in the twenty-first century are leaders who embrace inquiry and avoid isolation in all of its forms. The leadership strategies outlined here will significantly improve the school and district leader's ability to impact their organization in a positive and meaningful way.

TODAY IS A GOOD DAY TO AVOID ISOLATION

1. Today is a good day to attend a meeting and focus specifically on being an active listener. There is no communication without listening. There is no learning without listening. When leaders listen, their ability to ask the right kinds of questions increases. When leaders are active listeners, increased respect and trust will emerge from everyone else in the organization.
2. Today is a good day to meet with stakeholders on their turf. Go to them. Leaders who go out into the community and engage with constituents and stakeholders outside of the school building will always benefit from the relationships that are established as a result of that type of outreach.
3. Today is a good day to read and learn something new. Tier 1 leaders take the time each day to make sure management activity is occurring and running smoothly. Tier 2 and Tier 3 leaders take the time each day to increase their expert power. What gets prioritized and monitored gets done. Leaders who place a premium on learning are leaders who do, in fact, learn.
4. Today is a good day to sign up for a Twitter chat. In today's age of social media and online learning, the ability to grow intellectually is always available to the leader and the leadership team. On any given day, at any given time, there are a multitude of free online learning opportunities available. High-impact leaders take advantage of those opportunities.

5. Today is a good day to job-shadow. Understanding the complexity, benefits, and challenges of jobs other than one's own is critical in understanding how leadership decisions may impact other segments of the organizations. Whether the job to be shadowed resides well below the job function of the leader or well above, there is still much to be learned.
6. Today is a good day to start a "to learn" list instead of a "to do" list. Leaders are, by their very nature, doers. However, the leader must also be an accomplished listener and a relentless learner. Learning doesn't just happen by accident. Learning requires action and commitment.
7. Today is a good day to get out of the office for an extended period of time. With today's technology, there is no reason for the leader to be office bound. It is easy for colleagues to find and communicate with the leader regardless of location or time of day. In fact, no matter where the leader is or what the leader is doing, the work of the office—whether it's done through e-mails, phone calls, or texts—will follow.
8. Today is a good day to articulate the "big mission" to both internal and external stakeholders. It is easy, and a leadership trap, to get bogged down in the day-to-day activities of school management. While a well-managed school is a prerequisite for overall school success, it is not sufficient for, or synonymous with, school success. It is the big, audacious, difficult goals that must be attended to on a daily basis. High-impact leaders must first understand what the big mission actually is, and then be able to articulate and model that mission on a daily basis. Don't just assume that everyone understands and remembers why the school exists in the first place. Don't just assume that everyone understands and recognizes what success, at the highest level, should really look like.

Chapter Fifteen

Sustaining Tier 3 Leadership

For many leaders, developing and maintaining the skills necessary to be a high-performing manager, a technical expert, and a mission-driven team builder can be an overwhelming task. The ability to sustain the energy and commitment needed to function in all of these leadership capacities can be overwhelming. The ability to find balance and a set of behaviors that lead to sustained excellence over time is not just critical for the leader, but for the overall health of the organization, as well (Goleman & Lueneburger, 2010).

Too often organizations find themselves dealing with the many challenges that come from unplanned, and often unnecessary leadership succession. When there is no sustainability in place by and for high-performing leaders, there will also be no sustainability in place for maintaining student learning or the ability to sustain organizational success (Hargreaves & Fink, 2004).

The ability to find balance between work and home; the ability to slow down, to pause; the ability to accept failure as a likely outcome for any one initiative, just as success is, all of these are key, to not only leadership sustainability as a person, but leadership sustainability as a team. These sustaining skills involve not only how the leader treats the work, but also how the leader treats the team and him or herself. These sustainability behaviors can be practiced and attended to if they are recognized and prioritized.

Critical to sustainability as a mission-driven leader is the ability to recognize that leadership is a team sport, that leadership is fundamentally about building and sustaining relationships, and that a sense of humor and perspective is a critical component of individual and organizational health.

IT'S ALL ABOUT THE TEAM

High-impact leadership is always the result of the work of a committed team of leaders and followers. The more leaders can build, support, expand, and empower a team of leaders, the more likely the work of the leader will be sustained over time, and the more likely the leader will be able to sustain their own passion for the work. If the burden of leadership at all levels, in all areas, for all measures of success and impact, fall only on the shoulders of one leader, the weight of that responsibility and the reality that the work is too complex for any one individual to master, all but ensures organizational failure in the long run.

Leaders who build sustainable organizational structures have large, empowered teams functioning and supporting all levels of the organization. When leaders build teams, they are building capacity. When leaders build capacity, they are building sustainability.

IT'S ALL ABOUT RELATIONSHIPS

At its core, Tier 3 leadership is relationship leadership (Popper, 2004). Without positive, trusting relationships, there cannot be a team in any true sense of the word. Without relationships that allow for open communication and critical analysis of progress and process, complex endeavors and difficult challenges cannot be met.

It is one thing for the leader to develop positive trusting relationships with all of the colleagues and stakeholders who support or benefit from the work of the organization. It is another thing for the leader to be able to maintain positive, open communication and trust with those members of the organization or those external stakeholders who do not agree with the leader.

It is very important for the leader to balance what is needed to serve the mission and serve one's own needs. In the case of the leader's relationship with him/herself, it is a question of balance. It's all about balance. Leaders who are able to sustain their work over time also take care of themselves over time.

IT'S ALL ABOUT A SENSE OF HUMOR AND PERSPECTIVE

Leadership in any sector is hard work. Educational leadership is certainly no exception. In fact, due to the complexity and conflicting expectations from parents, students, policymakers, and business leaders about what the fundamental purpose of educating should even be, education leaders face uniquely challenging and stressful jobs.

Education leaders work in environments of constant change and constant pressure. In most organizational sectors, success can be clearly measured. Quarterly profit margins, stock prices, and sales reports—all are concrete measurements of organizational success. In the education sector, however, there is not a national consensus on what success looks like for a twenty-first-century school leader.

For the many outcomes that are used to define school success, each school leader is expected to produce results. Markers such as assuring that every child is at the correct grade level; that every child graduates on time with the ability to choose any post-graduation path; that the system is producing high standardized test scores disaggregated by subject, by gender, and by ethnicity; that student conduct data demonstrates a safe and orderly environment; that parent satisfaction data is documented; that all graduates function as good citizens, and so forth are just some of the outcomes modern education leaders are expected to produce.

All of these indicators for success can be stressful when attempting to make a difference for even one child, let alone all of the students in the school or the district. Clearly, educators work in environments where victory, as a final summative event, never occurs. There is always another mountain to climb, another obstacle to overcome, another challenge to tackle. Leaders who work in these types of ambiguous environments are subject to great stress. Unless that stress can be recognized and managed, the likelihood of the leader sustaining excellence and a mission focus is low.

In modern education environments, leaders may be able to sustain management skill (Tier 1) over time. Leaders may even be able to sustain expert skill (Tier 2) over time. The ability to maintain a relentless focus on the mission through team building and interpersonal development for all stakeholders, however, does not occur without the leader, and the entire leadership team understanding the role of failure as a growth opportunity and the fundamental importance of humor and perspective as a critical safety valve for stress (Davis & Kleiner, 1989).

SUSTAIN LEADERSHIP THROUGH HUMOR

Leaders who are able to sustain a mission-driven focus and a team orientation are leaders who know how to laugh, how to have fun in the workplace. These leaders have a sense of humor and are not afraid to use humor in ways that are both self-deprecating and that help ease the daily tensions of the workplace. In short, these leaders recognize the power of humor to help sustain the organization. Humor binds teams of people together. Humor humanizes leaders. Where humor is part of the organization's culture, there is less likelihood that the leader or the organization as a whole will take itself too seriously, and there is a greater likelihood that the leader will be able to achieve organizational goals (Schnurr, 2008).

The ability to make fun of oneself, to find the humor in even the most stressful of circumstances and in the most absurd of situations, is a key component of leadership and organizational mental health. In too many of the situations that inevitably occur when working in volatile, uncertain, complex, and ambiguous environments, leaders, if not careful, can become overwhelmed, depressed, isolated, and fearful as a response to the magnitude of the mission. Having a sense of perspective and a sense of humor goes a long way in mitigating those tendencies.

SUSTAINING LEADERSHIP THROUGH FAILURE

In his TED Talk on education and creativity (Robinson, 2006), Sir Ken Robinson discusses the unhealthy stigma that modern educators, and the culture as a whole, place on any type of failure. In an era of hyperaccountability, failure becomes the worst thing, the most dangerous thing that can happen to a student, a teacher, a school. Because risk, at any level, implies the potential for failure, then it is a short organizational leap to the leadership position that risk also should be avoided at all costs.

For students, this means, among other things, an addiction to the value of the grade above the value of learning itself. In order to always get the "correct" answer, the correct grade, the student's focus is not on inquiry or creativity, but instead on how the teacher wants the answer to look. The most common questions that are asked by students in this failure- and risk-averse educational environment are questions like, "Is this on the test?" or "How many pages would you like the answer to be?"

Sadly, one significant impact of avoiding risk and failure at all costs is the loss of creativity in the organization. Organizations that are not creative are not well equipped to lead in the twenty-first century. Organizations that do not embrace and support creative thought and action are unlikely to prosper in complex and ambiguous environments such as schools.

By demonizing failure at every level of the organization, the basic understanding of how learning and innovation actually occur are undermined. Making mistakes and learning from those mistakes is a core component of the learning process (Hattie & Timperley, 2007). We know that making mistakes is fundamental to learning and growing, and yet we still operate in too many settings, as if avoiding failure is the appropriate cornerstone of the teaching-learning process.

For all of the adults in the building, from first-year teachers to seasoned superintendents, the fear of failure as a driving organizational principle has equally damaging consequences for the overall health of the organization.

Fear breeds timidity. Fear breeds stress and paranoia. Fear limits both critical thinking and creative thinking. Wherever avoiding failure, at any level, is a high priority, achieving great and significant outcomes is a low probability.

By seeing failure as part of the learning and continuous improvement process, and by using failure as a way to learn and get better, as opposed to something to avoid, leaders can reduce the stress, the anxiety, within the workforce and in the student body (Sitkin, 1992). High-stress environments cannot be sustained over time. Strategies that reduce stress increase sustainability. Minimizing the significance of failure is a key attribute of effective Tier 3 leadership.

IT'S ALL ABOUT FEEDBACK AND REFLECTION

In a short article entitled "5 Characteristics of a Culture That Values Growth and Development," Katie Martin (2017) discusses the importance of building organizational structures that value and support opportunities for everyone in the organization to reflect on the growth of the organization itself and the individuals within the organization. The ability to self-reflect allows the organization to process both success and failures as part of the normal change process.

Rather than seeing failure as the end of the journey, or not being able to see success because it is often intermittent or incremental, leaders who build reflection as a core daily component of the leadership process are much more likely to sustain a positive, continuously improving climate within the organization.

In addition, the ability to have formal opportunities for everyone within the organization to both give and receive feedback is another critical way to maintain positive momentum, and thus personal as well as organizational sustainability over time (Drago-Severson, 2012). When leaders are checking in with all of the stakeholders on a formal and informal basis, and allowing for frank and open feedback regarding what is working and what is not working, a sense of empowerment and connectedness between leaders and followers is much more likely to be established.

Organizations with great feedback loops are less likely to have anxious or disconnected employees. Quality feedback does not just occur. There are multiple traps and challenges regarding effective feedback for both the giver and the receiver. In the book *Thanks for the Feedback: The Science and Art of Receiving Feedback Well*, Stone and Heen (2014) present a clear picture of the challenges and opportunities inherent in any feedback system.

While recognizing that every feedback system, no matter how well devised and no matter how well trained and coached the organization's members are, will have limitations and challenges, no organization can truly build a culture of learning without building a culture that supports and values feedback in all of its forms.

IT'S ALL ABOUT MOVING WHO OWNS THE MISSION FROM THE LEADER TO THE ORGANIZATION

Serving in a leadership capacity has many positive elements. The ability to make a significant difference, the ability to be part of a team working toward a common mission, and the ability to develop others are just a few of the many positive attributes of serving in the role of a leader. But leadership comes with a price, and the responsibilities of leadership are significant and can, if not handled with care, begin to impact leadership behavior and even the health of the leader.

When leaders act as if they are the only individuals who can sustain the mission and all of the activities that are involved in that process, long-term success is unlikely. The same is true for any efforts to create environments that are sustainable over a long period of time. Sustainability of the mission and the team is also a team sport. In short, sustainability is the responsibility of the organization, not of any one leader or small group of leaders who happen to have position power.

In order for mission sustainability to occur, the leadership team must also have in place all of the components of Tier 3 leadership discussed in this book. Some leaders get themselves to mission-driven behavior but don't build systems and teams that influence others to join in on the mission. When the leader moves on, the mission dies, because the mission was never truly owned by the stakeholders of the larger organization. Without a strategic plan designed specifically to address these issues and to consciously build mission sustainability into the team's work, the mission will falter as leadership teams inevitably move on to other jobs or retirement.

BURNOUT IS NOT A FUNCTION OF TIME ON THE JOB

It is a common occurrence in the field of education to hear colleagues speak of burnout. Teacher burnout and principal burnout are often the reasons given for an individual who is leaving the profession or losing the commitment to the mission or even the effort needed to complete the daily obligations of the job. *Webster's Dictionary* defines *burnout* as "exhaustion of physical or emotional strength or motivation, usually as a result of prolonged stress or frustration."

This notion of burnout as a function of time, of prolonged periods of stress, is common. Typically burnout is not associated with beginners on the job, but is seen as a result of individuals who have been on the job, and operating under pressure, for many years. Recent research however, suggests that burnout is as much a function of personality and attitude as it is of time (Katz, 2017).

Clearly, large numbers of leaders serve in highly stressful capacities for decades and never experience what would typically be defined as burnout. There are also always examples of leaders who quickly succumb to the pressures of the job, even after just a year or two. Katz's research suggests a causal link between leadership confidence, expert power, and burnout.

In short, the more a teacher, or a leader, is truly confident that they know and understand the job and how to do it well, and the more the individual feels they have the know-how, the expertise, to accomplish the job, the less job-related anxiety they will face. The less anxiety about overall job performance and capability the individual has, the less likely they are to experience what would typically be seen as on-the-job burnout.

In this context, one strategy for avoiding burnout includes a commitment to building and maintaining expert power. Leaders who remain lifelong learners, who are committed to maintaining all of the technical expertise needed for the job, are less likely to suffer from anxiety, stress, and burnout, than leaders who are not confident in their own expertise.

TODAY IS A GOOD DAY TO WORK ON SUSTAINING TIER 3 LEADERSHIP

1. Today is a good day to reflect on all that has been accomplished. Reflection matters. It is through reflection that leaders can gain a deeper understanding of what is working and what is not working.
2. Today is a good day to plan a social activity, a vacation, a celebration. The organization will successfully function without the leader when the leader has built and empowered teams of leaders. Leaders who believe they are irreplaceable are leaders who have not distributed leadership to others in any meaningful way.
3. Today is a good day to pause, even if for just a moment. Leaders who take the time to pause and relax each day are leaders who can sustain excellence over time. Leaders who don't have the time to relax are leaders who will quickly run out of time to lead.
4. Today is a good day to read something for pleasure. Look at all the reading that is occurring. How much of that reading is reading for information, is technical reading, or is reading directly related to the work? To sustain excellence over time, also read for pleasure.
5. Today is a good day to accept recognition for a job well done. Leaders are often excellent at recognizing the outstanding work of others while

reluctant to accept recognition themselves. When compliments and recognition come the leader's way, own them. They have been earned.

6. Today is a good day to exercise. Take thirty minutes, or even fifteen minutes, but build exercise into the daily schedule. If CEOs of Fortune 500 companies, governors, senators, and presidents can build daily exercise into their schedules, school leaders can do the same.
7. Today is a good day to engage in a hobby. Leaders with hobbies are leaders who are interested in more than just the work. Whether it is cooking, a sport, or model trains, there is something of interest for everyone outside of work. Find that area of interest and dedicate time toward that area.
8. Today is a good day to think about leadership succession planning. Everyone will be replaced someday. The question becomes, how does that replacement process occur? Is it random and spur of the moment, or is it the result of careful planning, mentoring, and selecting? Take some time to work with the team on succession planning.
9. Today is a good day to work with the leadership team on mission-sustainability activities. When teams are involved in identifying issues and coming up with solutions, the likelihood for success increases. The same is true in the area of increasing the likelihood of building the capacity for leadership sustainability over time and reducing the likelihood of leader burnout. Developing plans to ensure sustainability is a team challenge, not an individual challenge.
10. Today is a good day to laugh. The literature is clear: Leaders with a sense of humor, a sense of perspective, are more likely to be seen by others as approachable and part of the team, as well as more likely to avoid burnout. Cultivate a sense of humor. Don't take everything so seriously—particularly yourself.
11. Today is a good day to recognize that failure is a part of learning or achieving anything that is truly worthwhile. If you are not failing at something, you are not reaching high enough. Failure is not the worst thing that can happen to a leader or an organization. Not learning from failure is where the real danger lies.

Bibliography

Abdullah, J.B., & Kassim, J.M. (2011). Instructional leadership and attitude towards organizational change among secondary school principals in Pahang, Malaysia. *Procedia-Social and Behavioral Sciences*, 15, 3304–09.
Amabile, T.M., Schatzel, E.A., Moneta, G.B., & Kramer, S.J. (2004). Leader behaviors and the work environment for creativity: Perceived leader support. *The Leadership Quarterly*, 15(1), 5–32.
Ammons, D.N., & Newell, C. (1989). *City executives: Leadership roles, work characteristics, and time management.* SUNY Press.
Avolio, B.J. (1999). *Full leadership development: Building the vital forces in organizations.* Sage.
Bandura, A. (1993). Perceived self-efficacy in cognitive development and functioning. *Educational Psychologist*, 28(2), 117–48.
Barsh, J., Capozzi, M.M., & Davidson, J. (2008). Leadership and innovation. *McKinsey Quarterly*, 1, 36.
Bennett, N., & Lemoine, J. (2014). What VUCA really means for you. *Harvard Business Review*, 92(1/2).
Blasé, J., & Blasé, J. (2000). Effective instructional leadership: Teachers' perspectives on how principals promote teaching and learning in schools. *Journal of Educational Administration*, 38(2), 130–41.
Bligh, M.C., Pearce, C.L., & Kohles, J.C. (2006). The importance of self and shared leadership in team based knowledge work: A meso-level model of leadership dynamics. *Journal of Managerial Psychology*, 21(4), 296–318.
Botha, R.J. (2004). Excellence in leadership: Demands on the professional school principal. *South African Journal of Education*, 24(3), 239–43.
Browne-Ferrigno, T., & Muth, R. (2004). Leadership mentoring in clinical practice: Role socialization, professional development, and capacity building. *Educational Administration Quarterly*, 40(4), 468–94.
Brunetti, G.J. (2001). Why do they teach? A study of job satisfaction among long-term high school teachers. *Teacher Education Quarterly*, 28(3), 49–74.
Bush, T. (2007). Educational leadership and management: Theory, policy and practice. *South African Journal of Education*, 27(3), 391–406.
Cahill, M.L. (2006). Every student a leader. *Principal Leadership*, 6(5), 34–8.
Cain, S. (2017, March 26). Followers wanted. *The New York Times*.
Churms, S. (2016, November 11). Principal intern reflection #3. Volusia County, Florida.
Colwell, C.J. (2015). *Impact: How assistant principals can be high performing leaders.* Lanham, MD: Rowman & Littlefield.

Colwell, C. (2017). The class of 2030. *American School Board Journal*.
Conger, J.A., Kanungo, R.N., & Menon, S.T. (2000). Charismatic leadership and follower effects. *Journal of Organizational Behavior*, 747–67.
Copland, M.A. (2003). Leadership of inquiry: Building and sustaining capacity for school improvement. *Educational evaluation and policy analysis*, 25(4), 375–95.
Covey, S.R. (1989). *The 7 habits of highly effective people: Restoring the character ethic* (rev. ed.). New York: Free Press.
Crosbie, R. (2005). Learning the soft skills of leadership. *Industrial and Commercial Training*, 37(1), 45–51.
Davis, A., & Kleiner, B.H. (1989). The value of humor in effective leadership. *Leadership & Organizational Development Journal*.
Danielson, C. (2011). *Enhancing professional practice: A framework for teaching*. ASCD.
Dinham, S. (2013). The quality teaching movement in Australia encounters difficult terrain: A personal perspective. *Australian Journal of Education*, 57(2), 91–106.
Dirks, K.T. (2000). Trust in leadership and team performance: Evidence from NCAA basketball. *Journal of Applied Psychology*, 85(6), 1004.
Drago-Severson, E. (2012). The need for principal renewal. The promise of sustaining principals through principal-to-principal reflective practice. *Teachers College Record*, 114(12), n12.
DuFour, R. (2002). The learning-centered principal. *Educational Leadership*, 59(8), 12–5.
Evans, R. (1996). *The Human Side of School Change: Reform, Resistance, and the Real-Life Problems of Innovation*. The Jossey-Bass Education Series. San Francisco: Jossey-Bass.
Everard, K.B., Morris, G., & Wilson, I. (2004). *Effective school management*. Sage.
Fry, L.W. (2003). Toward a theory of spiritual leadership. *The Leadership Quarterly*, 14(6), 693–727.
Gardner, W.L., Avolio, B.J., Luthans, F., May, D.R., & Walumbwa, F. (2005). "Can you see the real me?" A self-based model of authentic leader and follower development. *The Leadership Quarterly*, 16(3), 343–72.
Gibson, S., & Dembo, M.H. (1984). Teacher efficacy: A construct validation. *Journal of Educational Psychology*, 76(4) 569.
Gillespie, N.A., & Mann, L. (2004). Transformational leadership and shared values: The building blocks of trust. *Journal of Managerial Psychology*.
Goddard, R.D., Hoy, W.K., & Hoy, A.W. (2000). Collective teacher efficacy: Its meaning, measure, and impact on student achievement. *American Educational Research Journal*, 37(2), 479–507.
Goleman, D., Boyatzis, R.E., & McKee, A. (2002). *The new leaders: Transforming the art of teaching into the science of results*. London: Little, Brown.
Goleman, D., Boyatzis, R.E., & McKee, A. (2013). *Primal leadership: Unleashing the power of emotional intelligence*. Harvard Business Press.
Goleman, D., & Lueneburger, C. (2010). The change leadership sustainability demands. *MIT Sloan Management Review*, 51(4), 49.
Greenleaf, R.K. (2002). *Servant leadership: A journey into the nature of legitimate power and greatness*. Paulist Press.
Griffith, J. (2004). Relation of principal transformational leadership to school staff job satisfaction, staff turnover, and school performance. *Journal of Educational Administration*, 42(3), 333–56.
Hargreaves, A., & Fink, D. (2004). The seven principles of sustainable leadership. *Educational leadership*, 61(7), 8–13.
Harris, A. (2003). Teacher leadership as distributed leadership: Heresy, fantasy or possibility? *School Leadership & Management*, 23(3), 313–24.
Harris, A. (2004). Distributed leadership and school improvement: leading or misleading? *Educational Management Administration & Leadership*, 32(1), 11–24.
Harris, A., & Lambert, L. (2003). *Building leadership capacity for school improvement*. McGraw-Hill Education (UK).
Haslam, S.A., Reicher, S.D., & Platlow, M.J. (2010). *The new psychology of leadership: Identity, influence and power*. Psychology Press.

Hatcher, R. (2005). The distribution of leadership and power in schools. *British Journal of Sociology in Education*, 26(2), 253–67.
Hattie, J., & Timperley, H. (2007). The power of feedback. *Review of Educational Research*, 77(1), 81–112.
Herrera, L. (2004). Plyler v. Doe. *Journal of Contemporary Legal Issues*, 14, 479.
Hunt, J.W. (2008). A nation at risk and No Child Left Behind: Déjà vu for administrators? *Phi Delta Kappa*, 89(8), 580–85.
Jameson, J., Ferrell, G., Kelly, J., Walker, S., & Ryan, M. (2006). Building trust and shared knowledge to communities of learning practice: Collaborative leadership in the JISC eLISA and CAMEL lifelong learning projects. *British Journal of Educational Technology*, 37(6), 949–67.
Kanter, R.M. (2000). When a thousand flowers bloom: Structural, collective, and social conditions for innovation in organization. *Entrepreneurship: The social science view*, 167–210.
Katz, Y. (2017). *The relationship between teachers' perceptions of emotional labour, teacher burnout, and teachers' educational level*. Presentation given at the 19th Annual International Conference on Education, Athens, Greece.
Kelley, R.C., Thornton, B., & Daugherty, R. (2005). Relationships between measures of leadership and school climate. Indianapolis: Chula Vista, 17.
Kluger, R. (2011). *Simple justice: The history of* Brown v. Board of Education *and Black America's struggle for equality*. Vintage.
Kotter, J.P. (2008). *Force for change: How leadership differs from management*. Simon and Schuster.
Kouzes, J.M., & Posner, B.Z. (2010). *The truth about leadership*. Soundview Executive Book Summaries.
Lee, P., Gillespie, N., Mann, L., & Wearing, A. (2010). Leadership and trust: Their effect on knowledge sharing and team performance. *Management Learning*.
Leithwood, K., Begley, P.T., & Cousins, J.B. (2005). *Developing expert leadership for future schools*. Routledge.
Leithwood, K., & Jantzi, D. (2000). The effects of transformational leadership on organizational conditions and student engagement with school. *Journal of Educational Administration*.
Leithwood, K., & Jantzi, D. (2008). Linking leadership to student learning: The contributions of leader efficacy. *Educational Administration Quarterly*, 44(4), 496–528.
Lundy, V., & Morin, P.P. (2013). Project leadership influences resistance to change: The case of the Canadian public service. *Project Management Journal*, 44(4), 45–64.
Lunenburg, F.C. (2012). Power and leadership: An influence process. *International Journal of Management, Business, and Administration*, 15(1), 1–9.
Martin, K. (2017). *5 characteristics of a culture that values growth and development*. https://katielmartin.com/2017/05/5.
Marzano, R.J., Waters, T., & McNulty, B.A. (2005*). School leadership that works: From research to results*. ASCD.
Mehra, A., Smith, B.R., Dixon, A.L., & Robertson, B. (2006). Distributed leadership in teams: The network of leadership perceptions and team performances. *The Leadership Quarterly*, 179(3), 232–45.
Merriam-Webster Collegiate Dictionary Online (11th ed.) (2003). S.v. "burnout." Retrieved from Credo database.
Meyer, A.E. (1967). *An educational history of the American people*, 2nd ed. McGraw.
Mumford, T.V., Campion, M.A., & Morgeson, F.P. (2007). The leadership skills strataplex: Leadership skill requirements across organizational levels. *The Leadership Quarterly*, 18(2), 154–66.
Noonan, J. (2004). School climate and the safe school: Seven contributing factors. *Educational Horizons*, 83(1), 61–5.
Ornstein, A., & Levine, D. (1993). *Foundations of education*. Houghton.
Pearce, C.L. (2007). The future of leadership development: The importance of identity, multi-level approaches, self-leadership, physical fitness, shared leadership, networking, creativity, emotions, spirituality and on-boarding processes. *Human Management Review*, 17(4), 355–59.

Pearce, C.L., & Conger, J.A. (2002). *Shared leadership: Reframing the hows and whys of leadership.* Sage.

Pearce, C.L., Hoch, J.E., Jeppesen, H.J., & Wegge, J. (2011). New forms of management.

Pierce, J.L., & Newstrom, J.W. (2003). *Leaders & the leadership process.* McGraw-Hill/Irwin.

Peng, W. J., McNess, E., Thomas, S., Wu, X.R., Zhang, C., Li, J.Z., & Tian, H.S. (2014). Emerging perceptions of teacher quality and teacher development in China. *International Journal of Educational Development*, 34, 77–89.

Perry, J.L., & Hondeghem, A. (eds.). (2008). *Motivation in public management: The call of public service.* Oxford University Press on Demand.

Pink, D. (2014). *Leadership and new principles of influence.* Presentation given at the Association for Curriculum and Supervision Development Conference, Los Angeles, CA.

Popper, M. (2004). Leadership as relationship. *Journal for the Theory of Social Behavior*, 34(2), 107–25.

Robertson, J. (2016). *Coaching leadership: Building educational leadership through partnership.* New Zealand Council for Educational Research.

Riggio, R.E., Chaleff, I., & Lipman-Blumen, J. (eds.). (2008). *The art of followership: How great followers create great leaders and organizations* (Vol. 146). John Wiley & Sons.

Rowe, A. (2003). *Diverse teams at work: Capitalizing on the power of diversity.* Society for Human Resource.

Schafer, M.S., & Taddicken, M. (2015). Opinion Leadership Mediatized Opinion Leaders: New Patterns of Opinion Leadership in New Media Environments? *International Journal of Communication*, 9, 22.

Scribner, J.P., Sawyer, R.K., Watson, S.T., & Myers, V.L. (2007). Teacher teams and distributed leadership: A study of group discourse and collaboration. *Educational Administration Quarterly*, 43(1), 67–100.

Semrud-Clikeman, M. (2016). *Research in brain function and learning: The importance of matching instruction to a child's maturity level.* American Psychological Association.

Senge, P.M. (2006). *The fifth discipline: The art and practice of the learning organization.* Broadway Business.

Senge, P.M. (2014). *The fifth discipline fieldbook: Strategies and tools for building a learning organization.* Crown Business.

Shamir, B., & Shamir-Eilam, G. (2017). Reflections on leadership, authority, and lessons learned. *The Leadership Quarterly*, 28, 578–83.

Sitkin, S.B. (nd). Learning through failure: The strategy of small losses. *Research in Organizational Behavior*, 14, 231–66.

Spillane, J.P. (2005). Distributed leadership. In *The educational forum* (Vol. 69, No. 2, 143–50). Taylor & Francis Group.

Stone, D., & Heen, S. (2014). *Thanks for the feedback: The science and art of receiving feedback well.* Penguin Books.

Schnurr, S. (2008). Surviving in a man's world with a sense of humor: An analysis of women leader's use of humor at work. *Leadership*, 43(3), 299–319.

Sweetser, K.D., & Kelleher, T. (2011). A survey of social media use, motivation and leadership among public relations practitioners. *Public Relations Review*, 37(4), 425–28.

The Dodge Idea. (1914). The waste basket waster. *Mill Supplies*, 39(7). Crawford Publishing Group.

Tredgold, G. (2017). Tweet.

Tschannen-Moran. (2009). Fostering teacher professionalism in schools: The role of leadership and trust. *Educational Administration Quarterly.*

United States, National Commission on Excellence in Education. Department of Education. (1983). *A nation at risk: The imperative for educational reform: A report to the Nation and the Secretary of Education*, United States Department of Education.

Wahlstrom, K.L., & Louis, K.S. (2008). How teachers experience principal leadership: The roles of professional community, trust, efficacy, and shared responsibility. *Journal of Educational Administration.*

Wageman, R. (2008). *Senior leadership teams: What it takes to make them great.* Harvard Business Press.

Weinberger, D. (2014). *Too big to know: Rethinking knowledge now that the facts aren't the facts, experts are everywhere, and the smartest person in the room is the room*. Basic Books.
White, R. (2008). Three characteristics of leadership-competence, consistency and character. Retrieved July 10, 2008.
Wright, B.E. (2007). Public service and motivation: Does Mission matter? *Public Administration Review*, 67(1), 54–64.
Zand, D.E. (1997). *The leadership triad: Knowledge, trust, and power*. Oxford University Press on Demand.
Zenger, J., & Folkman, J. (2002). *The extraordinary leader: Turning good managers into great leaders*. New York: McGraw-Hill.

About the Author

Christopher Colwell, EdD, is an associate professor and chair of the Education Department at Stetson University in DeLand, Florida. Dr. Colwell teaches teacher education and educational leadership education and serves as a consultant on P–12 leadership development. His research interests focus primarily on school leadership. He draws from forty years of work as a classroom teacher, an assistant principal, a principal at all levels of P–12 education—elementary, middle, and senior high school—and as a deputy superintendent prior to joining Stetson University. Chris was named the Secondary Principal of the Year for the state of Florida. He served as president of the Florida Organization of Instructional Leaders during his tenure as deputy superintendent for instructional services for the Volusia County, Florida, School District. Chris is the author of *Impact: How Assistant Principals Can Be High Performing Leaders*, published by Rowman & Littlefield in 2015.

www.ingramcontent.com/pod-product-compliance
Lightning Source LLC
Chambersburg PA
CBHW021844220426
43663CB00005B/391